Teacher's Handbook

ECCE ROMANI

A Latin Reading Program
Revised Edition

3
Home and School

Longman

Ecce Romani   Teacher's Handbook 3

ISBN 0 8013 0446 6
(78256)

Cover illustration by Judy Hans Price.

This edition of ECCE ROMANI is based on ECCE ROMANI A LATIN READING COURSE, originally prepared by The Scottish Classics Group © copyright The Scottish Classics Group 1971, 1982, and published in the United Kingdom by Oliver and Boyd, a Division of Longman Group. This revised edition has been prepared by a team of American and Canadian educators:
  Authors: Professor Gilbert Lawall, University of Massachusetts, Amherst, Massachusetts
  Consultants: Dr. Rudolph Masciantonio, Philadelphia Public Schools, Pennsylvania
    Ronald B. Palma, Holland Hall School, Tulsa, Oklahoma
    Dr. Edward Barnes, C. W. Jefferys Secondary School, Downsview, Ontario
    Shirley Lowe, Wayland Public Schools, Massachusetts

Acknowledgments:
  The authors of this edition of ECCE ROMANI would like to acknowledge the following for granting permission to publish literary extracts:
  Harvard University Press, for the material on pages 43–48 of this handbook, reprinted by permission of the publishers and the Loeb Classical Library from *Xenophon* by Socrates, translated by O.J. Todd (1922); *De Senectute* by Cicero, translated by William Armistead Falconer (1923); *Odes* by Horace, translated by C.E. Bennett (1914); *Institutio Oratoria* by Quintilian, translated by H.E. Butler (1920); *Dialogue on Oratory* by Tacitus, adapted from a translation by W. Peterson and M. Winterbottom (1914); *Brutus* by Cicero, translated by G.L. Hendrickson (1939); *Pro Lege Manilia* by Cicero, translated by H. Grose Hodge (1927); *Letters* by Seneca, translated by Richard M. Grummere (1917).
  The Oxford University Press, for the extract on page 42 of this handbook reprinted by permission of the publishers from *The Symposium or Drinking Party* by Plato, translated by B. Jowett (1920).
  The New American Library, New York, N.Y., for the material on pages 40–42, 47 of this handbook, reprinted by arrangement with the publisher from the *Satyricon* by Petronius, translated by William Arrowsmith (1959).

Longman
95 Church Street
White Plains, New York 10601

Associated companies:
Longman Group Ltd., London
Longman Cheshire Pty., Melbourne
Longman Paul Pty., Auckland
Copp Clark Pitman, Toronto
Pitman Publishing Inc., New York

ABCDEFGHIJ-CT-959493929190

Contents

Introduction to Book 3: Home and School

The major new grammar in the third book is the passive voice of all tenses of the verb in the indicative. Also treated are comparative and superlative adjectives and adverbs, deponent verbs, time and place constructions, and the present active participle. Imperfect and pluperfect subjunctive forms are introduced in the last chapters as a foretaste of what is to come in the fourth book. The cultural content of the stories focuses on dining in the first half of the book and on education in the second. A theme woven in among these major topics is that of the hazards and violence of life in the Roman world, both in the streets of Rome and on the high seas. Teachers should consult the Bibliography at the end of this handbook for a list of basic, highly recommended background and source books for the cultural topics. The cultural background readings grouped as the next to the last section of this handbook concentrate on dining, education, and piracy. Teachers should familiarize themselves with these readings and make use of them as frequently as possible.

There are 482 new words in the student's book; they are marked in the vocabulary at the end of the book with numbers indicating the chapter in which they first appear. English to Latin vocabularies for all of the English to Latin translation exercises in the chapters and review sections of the language activity book are provided at the back of this teacher's handbook. Also included are other word lists, one of basic words to be mastered in the course of the Latin program and one of verbs of which the principal parts are to be mastered as students progress through the chapters of the third student's book.

A new feature incorporated into this teacher's handbook will be found in frequent recommendations for written work in English, usually involving essays or creative writing based on the cultural content of the material in the student's book. It has always been a contention of Latin teachers that study of Latin improves English language skills. Such improvement may derive partly from formal word study incorporated into the Latin course. Teachers should encourage students to use Latin-based English words in their spoken and written English, and teachers should pay special attention to correct use of the more difficult, polysyllabic English words derived from Latin elements. Teachers should also encourage good written English. The Latin teacher can make a special contribution here by urging students to incorporate, into their written English, elements of structure and style that are pointed out in the notes in the teacher's handbooks on the Latin reading passages and that can be carried over into effective written English.

In addition to this attention to diction and structure, teachers should also avail themselves of the content of the stories and the cultural material as a basis for both oral discussion in class and formal written work. Particularly important here are comparisons and contrasts between the elements of ancient Roman culture and the culture of the students' world; the questions and topics that we suggest in the teacher's notes frequently address these matters. We strongly recommend that teachers take advantage of these suggestions for written work and incorporate an English writing component into their teaching of the Latin course.

A cumulative review of books 1–3 is included at the beginning of the fourth teacher's handbook and may be used either after book 3 at the end of Latin I or before beginning book 4 in Latin II.

Teaching Notes

CHAPTER 27: GOING SHOPPING

Student's Book

1. a. Three passive forms are introduced in the story (**ferēbantur**, 15; **portābantur**, 16–17; and **portātur**, 17 and 20) as vocabulary items. The passive voice will be treated in the next chapter.
    b. The vivid or historic present (encountered but not discussed in Chapter 13; see the first teacher's handbook, Chapter 13, Student's Book, note 2) is used in lines 18–26 and is discussed in this chapter.
    c. The forms and use of the relative pronoun are consolidated.
    d. The story begins in Aurelia's bedroom but soon moves to the busy streets of Rome, as Aurelia and Cornelia go shopping in preparation for a dinner which will be the focus of attention in the stories through Chapter 32. In order to situate the domestic scene within its larger context of life in Rome, background is offered on townhouses and tenements, contrasting the living conditions of well-to-do families such as that of Cornelius with those of poorer Romans.
    e. Additional material on prefixes is presented as a continuation of the work on prefixes at the end of the second student's book (pp. 90–93).
2. Words to be deduced: **tremere** (3), **neglegentia** (4), **neglegēns** (5), **vocāre** (5), **inīre** (8), **invītāre** (10), **versus** (18), **recitāns** (19), and **flamma** (31). Form to be deduced: **portābantur** (16–17) from **ferēbantur** (15).
3. The relative pronoun has been used in the reading passages and exercises since the beginning of the course (**Cornēlia est puella Rōmāna quae in Italiā habitat**, 1:1–2) and will be quite familiar to students at this stage. As the story is read, attention should be paid to the relative pronouns, which appear in many forms: **quārum** (2), **quae** (2), **cui** (9), **quibus** (9), **cuius** (11), **quae** (18), **quae** (20), **quī** (20), **quōrum** (22), **quī** (24), **quō** (26), **quam** (28), and **quā** (29). After the note at the bottom of page 7 is studied and the following exercises have been completed, the teacher may wish to return to the story and have students identify each relative pronoun and explain its gender and number (dependent on its antecedent) and case (dependent on its use in its own clause).
4. Structures:
    a. Verb and subject inverted: **Crīnēs . . . cūrāb-** ant duae ancillae. . . . (1–2) and elsewhere in the story. Have students locate all examples.
    b. Anaphora:
    . . . **quārum altera . . ., altera. . . .** (2)
    Nunc cōnspicit poētam . . ., nunc mendīcōs . . ., nunc lectīcam. . . . (18–19)
    c. List: . . . **servī, mīlitēs, virī, puerī, mulierēs.** (16)
    d. Participial phrases (active):
    . . . **poētam versūs recitantem. . . .** (18–19)
    . . . **mendīcōs pecūniam petentēs. . . .** (19)
    . . . **servōs per viam festīnantēs. . . .** (22)
    e. Participial phrases (passive):
    . . . **neglegentiā . . . vexāta. . . .** (4)
    . . . **īrā commōtus. . . .** (26)
5. Vocabulary:
    a. The three 3rd declension nouns are i-stems: **crīnēs**, **glīs**, and **fīnis** (see the teacher's handbook for Chapter 17, Student's Book, note 13, for a discussion of 3rd declension i-stem nouns).
    b. The word **alter** was encountered as early as Chapter 1 in the sense "a second": **Etiam in pictūrā est altera puella** (1:4). It is included in the vocabulary list here to bring out the meanings "the one . . . the other" (of two).
6. Attention may also be paid to the following:
    a. partitives expressed with the genitive case (**quārum altera**, 2, and **quōrum alter**, 22) and with **ex** (or **ē**) + abl. with numbers (**ūnus ē lībertīs**, 30)
    b. **quod** "because" (3, 27), which should not be confused with the relative pronoun
    c. exclamatory **Quam . . . !** (5)
    d. the indefinites **quōsdam** (9), **quendam** (11), and **quīdam** (24). The full declension of the indefinite adjective is given on page 108. At some point the teacher should call students' attention to the fact that most forms of this adjective are simply those of **quī**, **quae**, **quod** plus -dam. Have students locate the forms that are different.
    e. the intensive **ipsa** (11), **ipsō** (23), **ipsīus** (30). The full declension of the intensive adjective is given on page 109. Students' attention should be directed to the forms that have endings different from those of regular 1st and 2nd declension adjectives; the forms may also be compared with those of **is**, **ea**, **id** and of **ille**, **illa**, **illud**.
    f. **ēlegantissimam** (19–20): This is the first superlative form in **-issimus** encountered in the course and is given in the vocabulary list. Comparative and superlative forms of adjectives will be introduced formally in Chapter 32.
    g. the interrogative pronoun: **Sed quid accidit?** (30). The forms of this pronoun may be compared with those of the relative pronoun; see page 109.
7. Attention should be paid to uses of the ablative case: cause (4, 26), manner (14), time when (23), agent (14–15, 16–17, and 20), and means or instrument (17). Full discussion of the ablative case with the passive voice should be left to the next chapters (see note on page 22 of the student's book).

8. Cultural background:
   a. For discussion of women's hair-dressing and hair styles, see *Rome: Its People, Life and Customs*, pp. 110–111; *Roman Life*, pp. 205–206 (with pictures); and *Daily Life in Ancient Rome*, pp. 167–168. Roman women were apparently often annoyed by what they regarded as the carelessness of the slaves who dressed their hair (see Martial, II.66.1–4).

   Advantage should be taken of the picture opposite page 5 for discussion of the implements used in hairdressing. For photographs of ancient hairpins and combs like those in the illustration, see *Roman Life*, p. 206, and for the glass perfume and water flasks, see *Roman Life*, p. 232.
   b. The **taberna** (11) which is Aurelia's destination for shopping for dormice is in the Forum Boarium, the cattle and meat market of Rome. See below, Chapter 29, Student's Book, note 6, and Chapter 30, Student's Book, note 3a.
   c. The Emperor's freedman (30), fat and ostentatiously reading a book while being carried, reclining, on his litter, is one of a class of freed slaves employed by the emperors in the civil service. Under Claudius some such men gained great wealth and power and came to be despised for their arrogance. Under Nero and subsequent emperors their power was greatly reduced.

9. Lines 18–21 of the story are particularly suitable for dictation because of the triple use of the relative pronoun (treated formally in this chapter), with ambiguous forms (**quae, quī**).

10. *The Relative Pronoun:* The chart of the forms of the relative pronoun brings together all of its forms along with their English meanings, which often seem to cause students trouble. Teachers may wish to discuss in more detail the relationship between the antecedent and the relative pronoun and the dependence of the *case* of the relative pronoun on its use in its own clause. The examples given on page 7 should be carefully analyzed, and special attention should be paid to the relative pronouns in the following exercises (27b, c, and d). Teachers may then return to the story and have students identify and explain the relative pronouns used in it (see note 3 above).

11. Exercise 27b:
   a. In No. 2, note the passive participial phrase, **multīs rēbus sollicita**.
   b. In No. 4, **ruīna** is to be deduced.
   c. In No. 5, **grunnīre** is to be deduced. The word is onomatopoetic.

12. Exercise 27d:
   a. In No. 1, **celerrimī** is to be deduced from the superlative adverb **celerrimē** introduced in Chapter 14.
   b. In Nos. 2 and 3, **sēcum** and **quibuscum** are to be deduced from **mēcum** in the story (line 6);

the teacher should call attention to the **cum** in these compound forms.

13. **Sententiae** from ancient sources will be quoted frequently in the student's book and are intended to accompany the subject matter of the story, the new vocabulary, or the grammar. The **sententiae** quoted after Exercise 27d illustrate uses of the relative pronoun. The first example shows a relative pronoun with a noun (**cōnsilium**) as its antecedent. The second has a pronoun (**id**) as its antecedent. In the third example, there is no stated antecedent; the pronoun **is**, "he," could be supplied. Students should become aware that antecedents are often not expressed in Latin.

14. The **īnsulae** or tenements of Rome have already been introduced in the second student's book (page 77); see the second teacher's handbook, Chapter 24, Student's Book, note 14a. For further information on town houses and tenements, see the following:
   a. *Roman Towns*, "Streets, Houses and Shops," pp. 21–28.
   b. *The Roman House*, "Insulae and Cenacula," pp. 9–15, and "The Domus," pp. 16–46, and the accompanying *Aspects of Roman Life Folder A* (white card 5.8, "Private Houses: the Domus"; yellow source card 1.13; plan sheet 3.3; and model sheet 4.1: all on building a **domus**).
   c. *Rome: Its People, Life and Customs*, "The Roman House," pp. 54–69.
   d. *Daily Life in Ancient Rome*, "Houses and Streets," pp. 22–51.
   e. *Roman Life*, "Roman Houses," pp. 72–91 (richly illustrated).
   f. *Houses, Villas and Palaces in the Roman World*, Chapters II–IV for detailed treatment of the **domus** and **īnsula**.
   g. The cultural background readings at the end of this teacher's handbook contain extracts from Tacitus' account of the Great Fire of A.D. 64. We recommend, however, that it not be introduced to the students at this point in Chapter 27 but rather at the end of Chapter 28, with other material on the hazards of life in Rome. See below, Chapter 28, Student's Book, notes 12e and f.

15. *PREFIXES II: More Compound Verbs:* Many new compound verbs appear in this grammar note and accompanying exercises. Some of them will appear later in the student's book, and some will not. It is not necessary that students learn all of the words presented here at this time. They should, however, come to understand the four basic principles introduced under the numbered headings. In addition, they should develop skill in deducing the meaning of the compound word from the meanings of the prefix and the base. Sometimes (particularly with **sub-**) this may require some thought, imagination, and attention to context. Students should be encouraged to think for them-

selves in deducing the meaning of compound verbs, even at the risk of making mistakes. For convenience, we list here all of the compound words that occur in this section, with their meanings.

accipere (ad + capiō), to take to oneself, receive
accurrere (ad + currō), to run towards, up to
addere (ad + dō), to add
addūcere (ad + dūcō), to lead on, bring
afferre (ad + ferō), to bring, bring to, bring in
appōnere (ad + pōnō), to put or place near
apportāre (ad + portō), to bring
arripere (ad + rapiō), to seize, snatch
auferre (ab + ferō), to carry away, take away
aufugere (ab + fugiō), to run away, escape
commovēre (con + moveō), to move, upset
compōnere (con + pōnō), to compose
conicere (con + iaciō) to throw (emphatic), guess
cōnsīdere (con + sedeō), to sit down
continēre (con + teneō), to hold together, contain
dēcidere (dē + cadō), to fall down
differre (dis + ferō), to carry apart, in different directions, to put off, to differ
effugere (ex + fugiō), to run away, escape
ēripere (e + rapiō), to snatch from, rescue
excipere (ex + capiō), to welcome
exclūdere (ex + claudō), to shut out
immittere (in + mittō), to send in, hurl at, hurl into, let loose, release
impōnere (in + pōnō), to place in or on, to put
importāre (in + portō), to bring in, to bring about
inclūdere (in + claudō), to shut in
irrumpere (in + rumpō), to burst in, attack
perficere (per + faciō), to do thoroughly, accomplish
reddere (red + dare), to give back
reficere (re + faciō), to repair
repetere (re + petō), to pick up, fetch, recover
retinēre (re + teneō), to hold back, keep
succurrere (sub + currō), to run under or to, to come to someone's aid, to come to mind
surripere (sub + rapiō), to snatch (from) under, to steal
trādere (trā + dō), to hand over

At the bottom of page 11 it is pointed out that **auferō** comes from **ab** + **ferō**. Students may be asked to try to construct the other principal parts of this verb (**auferre**, *abs*tulī, *abl*ātum); note that **ab** is used when the verb no longer begins with *f* and that **abs** is used before the *t* in the 3rd principal part. The students will meet **abstulit** in Exercise 27e, No. 7.

When doing Exercise 27f, students may be asked to give the infinitive of the simple verb to highlight the change that occurs in the medial vowel or diphthong when the prefix is added and the change of conjugation in some verbs.

Language Activity Book

1. Activity 27c provides practice in the use of the relative pronoun and also illustrates the point that relative clauses are statements or sentences subordinated within another statement or sentence. Careful attention must be paid to the rules governing the gender, case, and number of the relative pronoun (see note on page 7 of the student's book).

   Successful completion of this exercise requires that the students be able to translate the two given sentences, decide how to combine them, figure out the use of the pronoun to determine the case, recognize the antecedent, remember that number and gender are determined by the antecedent, and then recall the correct form of the relative pronoun.

   Many students may not be ready to take all of these steps *by themselves*. At first, they may need to be led through the logical, step-by-step process with appropriate questions from the teacher. Once the process has been learned through careful working out of a quarter or a third of the examples in Activity 27c, students should be able to do the remainder by themselves.

2. Activity 27e: An English to Latin vocabulary list for this and all other English to Latin translation exercises in the language activity book is included on pages 56–58 of this teacher's handbook. It may be duplicated and given to students as needed, and it may also be used for general English to Latin vocabulary review. The following is a sample translation of the paragraph in Activity 27e:

   In cubiculō ancillae Aurēliae crīnēs eius neglegenter pectēbant. In tablīnō lībertus multās epistulās scrībēbat. In culīnā concursābant servī quī cēnam parābant. Aliī senātōrēs in triclīniō recumbēbant, aliī in lectīcīs ā servīs ad iānuam ferēbantur. Cornēlius hospitēs in ātriō salūtābat. Līberī in hortō lūdēbant.

CHAPTER 28: FIRE!

Student's Book

1. a. The primary aims of this chapter are to present a formal definition of the passive voice and to tabulate the forms of the passive voice for the present, imperfect, and future tenses.
   b. The story continues from the ominous words at the end of the previous story and focuses on one of the hazards of tenement life in the city of Rome—fires. The pathos of the events, Cornelia's poignant sympathy, and Aurelia's sense of helplessness and resignation should provide sources of lively discussion of the disadvantages and dangers of city life and of its effects on city dwellers. These themes are also illustrated in readings at the end of the chapter from Juvenal and in selections from Pliny and Trajan given in the original Latin and accompanied by translations.

2. Meanings for the passive forms **aguntur** (7), **opprimuntur** (18), **opprimēminī** (21), **commoveor**

(22), **commovēris** (26), and **servābimur** (27) are given in the vocabulary. On the basis of the 3rd person plural form **aguntur** (7), students are expected to deduce the meanings of **efferuntur** (7), **trahuntur** (7—8), **ēiciuntur** (8), and **pōnuntur** (8).

3. Words to be deduced: **ēmittere** (1), **obscūrāre** (5), **īnfāns** (7), **efferre** (7), **spectāculum** (9), **miserābilis** (9), and **exstinguere** (15).

4. Structures:
   Anaphora: **Lacrimābant mulierēs . . . ; lacrimābant līberī. . . .** (9—10).

5. The passage contains a variety of pronouns and demonstrative adjectives that may be highlighted in preparation for consolidation of the forms of demonstrative adjectives and pronouns in Chapter 29:
   a. Personal and demonstrative pronouns: **eī** (3), **eōrum** (12), **nōs** (14, 18, 26, 27), **vōs** (21), **ego** (22), **eōs** (23), **eīs** (24), **id** (25), and **tū** (26).
   b. Demonstrative adjectives: **id** (2), **eī** (3), **hāc** (15), **hoc** (16), **hōs** (16), **huius** (17), **hī** (17), **hōs** (22), and **illō** (29).
   c. Relative pronouns: **quā** (1), **quī** (10, 11, 12), **quae** (15), and **cui** (25).
   d. Interrogative pronouns: **Quis . . . ?** (23) and **Quid . . . ?** (24).
   e. Reflexive adjective and pronoun: **suōs** (11) and **sē** (18).
   f. Distributive pronoun: **aliī . . . aliī. . . .** (12— 13).
   g. Intensive adjective: **ipsum** (5), **ipsae** (27), and **ipsō** (29).

6. Note the use of the historic present in the second paragraph:
   . . . **aguntur . . . efferuntur . . . trahuntur . . . ēiciuntur . . . pōnuntur. . . .** (7—8).

7. Notes on vocabulary and special usages:
   a. Students should be invited to try different translations of **vīs fūmī ac flammārum** (1—2). The phrase **vīs pulveris**, "a cloud of dust," appeared in 15:17.
   b. For **cum**, "when," with inverted temporal and main clauses (**Cornēlia . . . currēbat cum Aurēlia eī clāmāvit. . . .**, 2—3), see the second teacher's handbook, Chapter 21, Student's Book, note 7.
   c. **īnfirmī** (7): This word has been used earlier in the sense of "weak," "shaky" (4:10 and Exercise 24a, No. 3). Here the adjective is being used in a different sense, "frail," "infirm," and it serves as a substantive, "the infirm."
   d. Note the partitives: **aliī ex adstantibus** (12) and **ūnus ex adstantibus** (20).
   e. Students may be reminded that some 1st declension nouns such as **incola** (13, 16) are masculine in gender (see second teacher's handbook, Chapter 24, Student's Book, note 6).
   f. Ablative of means: **. . . flammīs . . . opprimuntur** (17—18), **. . . opprimēminī aut lapidibus aut flammīs** (21). Ablative of manner: **. . . magnō fragōre cecidērunt** (29).

8. The following **sententia** could also be taught in this chapter, along with the forms of the passive voice: **Ignis nōn exstinguitur igne** *Fire is not extinguished by fire* (Medieval maxim).

9. *VERBS: Active and Passive Voice:* Some students may ask why the passive voice exists, since the active voice is capable of expressing the same information that the passive is expressing. There are at least two advantages of the passive:
   a. It allows the receiver of the action to become the focal point of the sentence, when the doer of the action is of less importance or interest, e.g.:

   > The President was shot.
   > *rather than*
   > Someone shot the President.

   b. It allows an action to be expressed without naming the doer, e.g.:

   > The bribe money was handed over.

   It will be noted that in the verb paradigms **parāre** has been replaced by **portāre** in order to avoid possible double meanings in forms such as **parātus sum**, "I have been prepared" or "I am ready."

   In the paradigms it should be noted that an *e* appears where an *i* would be expected in **mitteris**, **iaceris**, **portāberis**, and **movēberis**. It should further be noted that only a macron and different placement of the accent distinguish **mitteris** (present tense) from **mittēris** (future tense). In the passive forms of **ferō**, the only irregularities are **ferris** (instead of **fereris**) and **fertur** (instead of **feritur**). The personal endings are regular.

10. In exercise 28b, No. 11, **memoria** is to be deduced.

11. **Versiculī**: "Fire," page 101
    Note the separation of the demonstrative adjective from its noun; **Haec . . . īnsula** (1). The passive infinitive (**servārī**, 2) will be introduced in Chapter 29 and is given here as a vocabulary item.

12. *Hazards of City Life*
    a. Suetonius (*Augustus* XXX) describes Augustus' establishment of fire brigades as follows:

    > He divided the area of the city into regions and wards, arranging that the former should be under the charge of magistrates selected each year by lot, and the latter under "masters" elected by the inhabitants of the respective neighborhoods. To guard against fires he devised a system of stations of night watchmen (**vigilēs**).

    > —tr. J. C. Rolfe

    Trimalchio's dinner party, at which his funeral is rehearsed, ends with the irruption of the local fire brigade:

    > The trumpeters broke into a loud funeral march. One man especially, a slave of the undertaker who was the most decent man in the party, blew such a mighty blast that the whole neighborhood was roused. The watch (**vigilēs**), who were patrolling the streets close by, thought Trimalchio's house was alight, and suddenly burst in the door and began with

water and axes to do their duty in creating a disturbance. My friends and I seized this most welcome opportunity . . . and took to our heels as quickly as if there were a real fire.

—tr. W. H. D. Rouse

For further details on the **vigilēs**, see the entry in *The Oxford Classical Dictionary*, pp. 1120–1121.

b. In working with the passages in Latin and English on page 18, students should be invited to make as many connections as possible between the Latin and the translation. We suggest having a student read the translation aloud and then having another student read the Latin aloud. The teacher may then ask students to locate words and phrases in the Latin that correspond to key words and phrases in the translation. In discussing the passages, reference should be made to both the Latin and the English, with an increasing emphasis on the Latin. The following words are especially important for any discussion of the passages, and their specific meanings are given here:

sīpō *or* **sīphō, -ōnis** *(m)* (Greek loan word): A water-hose and apparatus for forcing water through it under pressure. Cf. English *siphon*.

hama, -ae *(f)* (Greek loan word): A water-bucket used in fire-fighting.

collēgium, -ī *(n)*: A group of people gathered formally for a common purpose, a club, board, society, guild, college

faber, fabris *(m)*: Craftsman, workman of any sort, (here) firefighter

factiō, factiōnis *(f)*: A grouping of people for social or political purposes, faction, (often with negative connotations) clique, cabal, group of conspirators or revolutionaries

hetaeriae, -ārum *(f pl)* (Greek loan word; the base of the word means "comrade," "companion"): Social group, political club

ut et ipsī inhibeant: Literally, "so that they themselves may check (the fires)," presumably by making use of the equipment that Trajan recommends should be provided, hence the translation in the text, "to make use of it for themselves."

c. Questions on the passages from Pliny and Trajan:

Does Pliny's request seem reasonable?

What is Pliny's main concern?

What is Trajan's main concern?

Will Trajan's recommendations provide a satisfactory solution to the problem with which Pliny is concerned?

d. Further topic for discussion or written work: Only extracts of these two letters are printed in the student's book. Pliny's letter also contains the following:

It (the fire) was fanned by the strong breeze in the early stages, but it would not have spread so far but for the apathy of the populace; for it is

generally agreed that people stood watching the disaster without bestirring themselves to do anything to stop it.

Trajan's letter concludes as follows:

. . . and to instruct property owners to make use of it, calling on the help of the crowds which collect if they find it necessary.

—tr. Betty Radice

Using the story at the beginning of Chapter 28, the above extracts from the letters of Pliny and Trajan, and (if possible) a recent newspaper account of an actual disaster at which bystanders either did or did not lend help, students may be asked to discuss (orally or in the form of a written essay) the extent to which and the circumstances in which bystanders should lend help in situations such as these.

e. The cultural background readings at the end of this handbook contain Tacitus' description of the Great Fire of Rome in A.D. 64, accompanied by questions for class discussion or written assignment. We recommend that all or part of this description be read to or otherwise shared with students by the teacher.

f. For further information and additional activities, see *Roman Towns*, pp. 34–35, and the accompanying *Aspects of Roman Life, Folder A* (white cards 5.3, "Problems of Living in Rome," and 5.7, "Life in Rome *versus* Life in the City"; yellow source cards 1.5, "The Problems of Living in Rome"; 1.6, "The Great Fire of Rome"; and 1.7, "Rome after the Fire."

Language Activity Book

1. Activity 28b provides practice with the forms and meaning of the passive voice, in contrast to the active.
2. Activity 28c contrasts the use of active and passive verbs in sentences.

CHAPTER 29: PSEUDOLUS CAUGHT OUT

Student's Book

1. a. No major new grammatical points are introduced in the first story; one example of the future perfect passive is introduced in line 23 (also Exercise 29b, No. 5) in anticipation of Chapter 30. There is intensive practice throughout the chapter in dealing with passive verbs.

b. The dialogue in Exercise 29b introduces the present passive infinitive.

c. The rules for use of the ablative case (with and without the preposition **ā** or **ab**) with the passive voice are presented.

d. The forms of **is, ea, id; hic, haec, hoc;** and **ille, illa, illud** are tabulated for review, and their uses as both demonstrative adjectives and pronouns are illustrated.

   e. The story line is resumed with an account of how the slave bought the pig mentioned in line 10 of story 27. The focus on the clever slave and his bargaining in the marketplace provides a glimpse into Roman everyday life and may prompt discussion of similarities and differences between shopping then and now. Exercise 29g develops the theme of clients and patrons (see page 76 of the second student's book) in a dialogue between two patrons of Messalla who discuss a scheme to get themselves invited with their patron to Cornelius' dinner. The chapter ends with cultural background material on Roman meals.

2. Words to be deduced: **retinēre** (30; met previously in Exercise 27f, No. 3) and **multum** (14 as substantive, 27 as adverb or cognate accusative, and Exercise 29g, line 5 as adjective; previously this word has been used only in the plural, **multī, -ae, -a,** many)

3. The following minor points of grammar should be noted, but they should not be allowed to overshadow attention to the passive voice:

   a. The dative case is often used in Latin to indicate possession: . . . **servus quīdam cui nōmen est Pseudolus** (5–6). Be sure students understand the construction in its literal sense ("to whom there is the name Pseudolus"), but encourage freer translations such as "who has the name Pseudolus" or "named Pseudolus."

   b. **vidētur** (6): The passive of the verb **videō** frequently means "to seem" and is often accompanied by an infinitive and/or dative. This meaning of the passive of this verb was first encountered in 20:25–26, and two examples occur in the present story: 6 and 9–10.

   c. The genitive case is used to denote the indefinite value (as opposed to the specific price) of something: **'Quantī,' inquit Pseudolus, 'est illa perna?'** (8).

   d. **Quem porcum . . .?** (16): Note the use of the interrogative adjective, which has the same forms as those of the relative pronoun.

   e. The price for which a thing is bought or sold is in the ablative case: **'. . . tibi decem dēnāriīs eum vēndam.'** (20).

   f. The word **grātīs** (23) is a shortened form of **grātiīs,** the ablative plural of **grātia,** and is an ablative of price. It means literally "for (no reward but) thanks" and thus more freely "for nothing."

   g. **sibi** (30): This is the first appearance of the dative of the reflexive pronoun in the course.

4. Structures:

   a. Balanced sentences:
     Nōn servus sed mercātor esse vidētur. (6)
     Praedō quidem mihi vidēris, nōn lanius. (9–10)

   b. Interrupted phrase:
     . . . ad laniī tabernam. . . . (7)

   c. Condensed sentence:
     Vōs servī, nōn nōs laniī, rēctē praedōnēs vocāminī. (25–26)

5. The teacher should explain that Pseudolus' name is formed from the Greek word *pseudēs* "lying," "false" (cf. English *pseudo-*) and the Latin word **dolus,** "deceit," "deception." Pseudolus is the name of a tricky slave who plays the title role in one of Plautus' comedies. Teachers may wish to call attention to *pseudo-* as a prefix in English words. In addition to *pseudonym* and *pseudoscientific*, which should be familiar to all students, students studying science will be familiar with *pseudopod, pseudomorph,* and *pseudocarp* (all with useful Greek bases: *pod* "foot," *morph* "shape," "form," and *carp* "fruit").

6. **ad laniī tabernam** (7): The shop where Pseudolus buys the pig would be in the Forum Boarium or "Cattle Market" (**bo-,** from **bōs, bovis** + the adjectival suffix **-ārius**). This was located between the west end of the Circus Maximus and the Tiber River (see the map on page 17 of *Rome: Its People, Life and Customs* and pictures of the archaeological and architectural remains in the area in *Pictorial Dictionary of Ancient Rome,* Vol. I, pp. 411–417). To the northeast and also along the Tiber was the Forum Holitorium or "Vegetable Market" (**hol-** from **holus, holeris** + the nominal suffix **-tor,** denoting an agent, and the adjectival suffix **-ius**). For the remains in this area, see *Pictorial Dictionary of Ancient Rome,* Vol. I, pp. 418–423). Conveniently situated along the Tiber, these were the great market places for produce and meat.

7. Students may need to be reminded how much a **dēnārius** (21, 28) was worth (cf. teacher's notes to "Eavesdropping" in the second teacher's handbook, page 17, note 2). The basic unit of coinage was the **as** (genitive, **assis**); 2½ **assēs** = 1 **sēstertius** or **nummus;** 4 **sēstertiī** = 1 **dēnārius;** 25 **dēnāriī** = 1 **aureus.** We can get an idea of the purchasing power of the **sēstertius** by looking, for example, at a soldier's rate of pay. Near the end of the first century A.D., a Roman solider in the ranks received 100 **sestertiī** or 25 **dēnāriī** a month. From this he had to buy his own food. Five **modiī** of wheat, the staple diet, was a month's supply. This cost five **dēnāriī,** or one-fifth of the solider's monthly wage. So, the **lanius** wants to charge an amount for his pig that could buy a two-month supply of grain for a solider. For further information on prices in ancient Rome, see *Aspects of Roman Life Folder A,* yellow card 1.14. "The Cost of Living."

8. Lines 18–20 are particularly suitable for dictation because of the various uses of the ablative case contained in them.

9. In Exercise 29b, the sentences are not drawn straight from the story; there are two changes of tense and three of person, all involving practice with passive forms. In No. 3, the future tense must be used in both clauses (future more vivid condition). In No. 5, the future perfect passive must be used, as it is in the story (line 23).

10. *Demonstrative Adjectives and Pronouns:* The charts of the demonstrative adjectives and pronouns bring together all of the forms of these words, which have been encountered frequently in the stories and exercises. The forms of **hic** and **ille** have already been tabulated in Chapter 25 (see the second teacher's handbook, Chapter 25, Student's Book, note 9; and see below, Language Activity Book, note 4, for a suggested learning activity for demonstrative adjectives and pronouns).

   The term *demonstrative* may be defined from its Latin etymology: **dēmōnstrō** (1), "to point out," "to show." In discussing the use of these words (in particular, **is**, **ea**, **id**) as pronouns, teachers may wish to review the personal pronouns of all three numbers, singular and plural (see the second teacher's handbook, Chapter 21, Student's Book, note 14c, and the tabulation of personal and demonstrative pronouns on page 109 of the third student's book). In Exercise 29g, special note should be taken of the distinction between the adjectival and pronominal uses of **is**, **hic**, and **ille**.

11. **Versiculī:** "A Shrewd Businessman," page 101
    Note the alliteration of p-sounds in the first line and the effective juxtaposition of **ōlim** and **nunc** in the second.

12. Roman Meals
    For further information on the topics treated here, see:
    a. *Roman Family Life*, "Daily Life," pp. 47–54, for a description of a typical day in Rome, including meals.
    b. *The Roman House*, pp. 31–36, for photographs, plans, and reconstructions of **triclīnia**.
    c. *Rome: Its People, Life and Customs*, "The Banquet," pp. 92–99, for the **triclīnium** and dining customs.
    d. *Roman Life*, "Meals of the Day," pp. 224–239, richly illustrated.
    e. *Daily Life in Ancient Rome*, pp. 263–276, for Roman dinners.

    A small bulletin board display with pictures of banquets and guests would be appropriate during this and the next chapters. Pictures may be gleaned from old texts and newspapers, and pictures of previous banquets held at the school can be displayed. For suggestions about mock Roman banquets, see the notes below to *Recipes and Menus* at the end of Chapter 31.

Language Activity Book

1. In addition to practice with passive verbs and the ablative of agent, Activity 29a involves some of the minor grammatical points mentioned above in note 3 to the student's book. The following are sample answers to the Latin questions:
   1. Iocus audiēbātur ab eīs quī in culīnā erant.
   2. Pseudolus rogāvit, "Quantī est illa perna?"
   3. Magnum pretium audītur.
   4. Minimē! Nēmō in hāc viā meliōrem carnem habet.
   5. Sī Pseudolus multum emet, pretium minuētur.
   6. Porcus ā laniō ipsō cūrābātur.
   7. Lanius senātōrī Rōmānō porcum vēndere vult.
   8. Servī rēctē praedōnēs vocantur.
   9. Octō dēnāriīs porcus et lepus Pseudolō trāduntur.
   10. Aurēlia in animō habet Pseudolum ad vīllam rūsticam mittere.

2. Activities 29b and c give practice with the present passive infinitive. The following are sample translations of the English sentences in Activity 29c:
   1. Cornēlius raedam ē fossā extrahī iussit.
   2. Aurēlia porcum pinguem emī volēbat.
   3. Porcus ā laniō captārī nōlēbat.
   4. Aurēlia Pseudolum pūnīrī vult.
   5. Pseudolus in urbe retinērī volēbat.

3. Activity 29d is an extension of work with the passive voice in Exercise 29e in the student's book. Here the student must transform the direct objects into subjects as they change the verbs from active to passive. The subject of the original sentence becomes an ablative with or without **ā** or **ab**. If students have trouble with these transformations, they should go back and study the examples in Exercise 29e in the student's book.

4. Note that in Activities 29e and f most of the substitutions involve forms of the demonstrative adjectives and pronouns with endings that are different from those of the nouns they replace. In learning the forms of these pronouns, as with the forms of the relative pronoun in Chapter 27, students should pay particular attention to the forms that have different endings from those of nouns. But, students should also note that *many* of the endings of the demonstrative adjectives and pronouns are similar to 1st and 2nd declension endings. Even the neuter accusative singular is easy to remember if the students are reminded that the nominative and accusative are always the same in the neuter. (Compare Activities 27a and b; the teacher may wish to conduct a similar activity in the classroom for demonstrative adjectives and pronouns, using charts to compare the forms with those of typical 1st, 2nd, and 3rd declension nouns.)

5. Activity 29g: For No. 5, students should be reminded that the partitive idea after numbers is expressed with **ex** or **ē** with the ablative and not with the genitive. The following are sample translations of the sentences:
   1. Magnus cachinnus ē culīnā ā Marcō et Sextō audiēbātur.
   2. Ille porcus per iānuam in culīnam dūcēbātur.
   3. Hic melior porcus ā Pseudolō emēbātur, quod Aurēlia eī satis pecūniae dederat.
   4. Hic lanius illum porcum decem dēnāriīs vēndet.
   5. Duo modo ē servīs illō iocō dēlectābantur.

6. Ille mercātor hunc pinguem porcum ā Pseudolō abdūcī iussit.
7. Aurēlia in animō habet Pseudolum punīre et ad vīllam rūsticam mittere.
8. Iubēbitne umquam Cornēlius Pseudolum procācem ad vīllam rūsticam mittī?
9. Pseudolus in urbe manēbit et ā dominō ad Forum mittētur, ubi aliquid parvō pretiō emī volet.

CHAPTER 30: PREPARATIONS FOR DINNER

Student's Book

1. a. The aims of this chapter are to introduce and explain the passive voice of the perfect, pluperfect, and future perfect tenses. Three examples are translated in the vocabulary: **invītātī erant** (1), **allāta erat** (8–9), and **cōnfecta erit** (16). From these examples students are to deduce **ēmptus erat** (3), **missī sunt** (3), **comparāta sunt** (5), **positī erant** (9), and **salūtātī sunt** (18). After having been given the translation of **invītātī erant** (1), students should have no trouble with **ēmptus erat** (3), which should be easily recognizable as a corresponding form in the singular. The next form, **missī sunt** (3), may be more difficult to deduce, but students who notice that the helping verb is now in the present tense will figure that this probably makes a difference in the time of the action. Some will translate "are sent," but those who remember that this would be **mittuntur** in Latin will see that **missī sunt** must be a past tense like **invītātī erant** (1) and will translate "were sent." Correct translation of the perfect passive ("were sent" rather than the tempting "are sent") is extremely important, and we accordingly invite students and teachers to linger over deducing the first example of this tense rather than giving it as a vocabulary item.
   b. Final preparations for the long awaited dinner are made, and the guests arrive. Mention of the mythological subjects of the pictures that decorate the walls of the **triclīnium** gives the teacher an opportunity to retell these and other mythological stories or to introduce them to students in versions from the ancient authors in English translation. The satirical and mocking description of the arrival of the guests at Trimalchio's dinner party may also be read as a contrast with the simple formalities of Cornelius' household.
2. Words to be deduced: **ornātus** (10) and **addūcere** (12; met previously in Exercise 27e, No. 2). Students will deduce the basic meaning of **ornātus** from its English derivative, *ornate*, but they should also be led to associate it with **ornāmenta**, "furnishings," met in 28:8 to arrive at a translation such as "well furnished."
3. Notes on vocabulary and special usages:

   a. **in Forō** (2): i.e., the Forum Boarium or general cattle and meat market. **in Forum** (3): i.e., the Forum Holitorium or produce market. See above, Chapter 29, Student's Book, note 6.
   b. **. . . cum . . . invītāvit. . . .** (5): Latin uses the perfect indicative in the protasis of present general conditional or temporal sentences; translate with the present tense in English: ". . . whenever a Roman senator invites. . . ." there is no need to stress this usage, but if it is mentioned it may be pointed out that this is another example of a linguistic usage in Latin that is quite different from English. Students may be reminded that certain linguistic features are unique to specific languages.
   c. Alliteration: **. . . culīnā cibus coquēbātur. . . .** (7).
   d. **in medium triclīnium** (8): "into the middle of . . ."
   e. Distributive adjective: **In aliā pictūrā . . . , in aliā . . . , in aliā. . . .** (11–12). Translate "In *one* picture . . . , in *another* . . . , in *another.*" Cf. 27:1–2 and 28:12–13.
   f. **nōna hōra** (14): about 3 P.M. For the Roman division of the day into twelve equal hours, see the second teacher's handbook, Chapter 9, Student's Book, note 4.
4. The pictures on the walls of Cornelius' dining room (10–13) may give rise to discussion. The story of Hercules and Cerberus is already familiar to students from Review V in the second student's book. They will read of Orpheus' descent to the underworld in Review VII after Chapter 31. The three scenes mentioned here are shown in the illustration on pages 32–33 with a fourth scene, that of Europa and the bull. For versions of these stories by Roman authors, the teacher may consult the following:
Hercules and Cerberus: Seneca, *Hercules furens* 782–829.
Charon: Vergil, *Aeneid* VI. 295–330.
Orpheus and Eurydice: Vergil, *Georgics* IV. 453–527 and Ovid, *Metamorphoses* X. 1–77.
Europa and the bull: Ovid, *Metamorphoses*, II. 833–875.
These stories are retold and discussed in many modern books on mythology, such as the following (arranged in ascending order of sophistication):
   a. *Mythology:* Hercules and Cerberus, pp. 233–234; Orpheus and Eurydice, pp. 138–142; Europa and the bull, pp. 100–105.
   b. *Myths and Their Meaning:* Hercules and Cerberus, p. 166; Charon, pp. 128–129; Orpheus and Eurydice, pp. 133–138; Europa and the Bull, pp. 36–38.
   c. *Myths of the Greeks and Romans:* Orpheus and Eurydice, pp. 304–311.
   d. *Mythology and You:* Hercules and Cerberus, p. 231; Orpheus and Eurydice, pp. 171–175; Europa and the bull, pp. 239–241.
   e. *Classical Mythology:* Hercules and Cerberus, pp. 392–394; Mercury (Hermes) and Charon, pp. 279–281; Orpheus and Eurydice, pp. 282–292. Europa and the Bull, pp. 297–299.
   The pictorial decorations in Roman houses were murals or frescoes painted directly onto the plaster of the walls when still damp. Teachers may wish to

bring in picture books or slides of Pompeian houses to illustrate this kind of decoration. Contrasts could be drawn with interior decoration of contemporary homes. It might be of interest to the students to know that images of death and the underworld were common in Roman dining rooms due to a belief that such grim reminders would help the individual appreciate more the pleasures of living. See *Rome: Its People, Life and Customs*, p. 97, and Petronius, *Satyricon* (34), in which a skeleton is brought in during the banquet to remind the guests of impending death and urge them to "live it up" while alive.

5. With the arrival of the guests for Cornelius' dinner, the teacher may invite students to compare Petronius' description of the arrival of guests at Trimalchio's banquet, a translation of which is included in the cultural background readings at the end of this handbook (pp. 40−42).

6. *VERBS: Perfect, Pluperfect, and Future Perfect Passive:* Eight examples of verbs in these tenses in the passive voice are included in the story (see note 1 above). After translating and discussing these forms in context and after examining the further examples in the middle of page 28, students will usually have discovered the rules for themselves and will be eager to state them. The charts of forms on pages 28 and 29 and the following notes should serve merely to confirm what the students have already discovered for themselves.

The neuter endings for the participles in the 1st and 2nd persons singular and plural are not included in the charts, because the subject of a sentence using a passive verb in these persons and numbers will normally be either a man or a woman. Students should be led to this conclusion through examples of sentences in English and Latin. This will reinforce rule No. 3 on page 29 about agreement of the participle with the subject in gender (and number). Students should then be led to see that the compound forms of the passive in these tenses must also be internally consistent and that both parts of the compound must agree. Thus, one would not say **portātus sunt** but either **portātī sunt** or **portātus est**. Exercise 30c and Activities 30a and b in the language activity book offer practice with agreement of subject, participle, and helping verb. Notice also the **sententia** on page 30 of the student's book.

Language Activity Book

The following is a sample translation of the dialogue in Activity 30d:

(Titus, patruus Marcī et Cornēliae, invītātus est ad cēnam quae senātōribus ā Cornēliō dabitur. Titus ā servō Polydōrō parātur.)

POLYDŌRUS: Sella, domine, tibi conducta est.

TITUS: Bene! Nunc adiuvā mē. Nōn rēctē est haec toga imposita. Ubi ambulō, sine dubiō cadet.

POLYDŌRUS: Quā in tabernā, domine, ēmpta est haec toga? Sordida est.

TITUS: Quid? Sordida? Servus quī hanc togam ēmit certē pūniētur. Aliam togam ad mē statim affer! (Sella quae ā servō conducta erat ad iānuam allāta est.)

UXOR TITĪ: Age, Tite. Sella adest. Sī sērō advēneris, ut bene scīs, ā frātre tuō reprehenderis.

TITUS (quī ē cubiculō exit): Ita vērō, illud sciō. Tandem parātus sum. Invēnī servum quī illam togam sordidam ēmit. Cum (*or* Ubi) redierō, eum pūniam.

(Titus in sellā cōnsīdit et celeriter per viās ā servīs portātur.)

WORD STUDY VIII

1. The aims of this section are:
   a. to explain the formation of some 4th declension nouns from verbs
   b. to present English derivatives of 4th declension nouns
   c. to provide further examples of compound verb formation and derivatives of those compounds

2. It should be pointed out to students that many 4th declension nouns are not related to verbs, e.g., **arcus, manus,** and **domus.**

3. Rather than dropping the **-us** ending, some English derivatives of 4th declension nouns retain it or replace it with silent -*e*, e.g.:
   consensus, from **cōnsēnsus, -ūs** (*m*) (from **cōnsentīre**)
   sense, from **sēnsus, -ūs** (*m*) (from **sentīre**)

4. In Exercise 1, students should give the noun in the nominative and genitive singular, with the gender designation. Students may need to consult a Latin dictionary for the correct meanings.

5. There are several interesting English derivatives from words in Exercise 3: *derision, course, conspectus, adit,* and *case.*

The following English expressions using 4th declension nouns might be mentioned: casus belli, in situ, lapsus linguae, and status quo.

6. In Exercise 4, students may need to consult a Latin dictionary for the meanings of the compound verbs and an English dictionary for the meanings of some of the English derivatives. Students should be encouraged to produce other English words derived from each compound, e.g., *commitment, committee, noncommittal,* and *commission.*

The verb **iaciō** and its derivatives may provide an opportunity for review of consonantal *i* in Latin. Although the Roman alphabet contained no *j*, the vowel *i*, when it occurs between vowels or before a vowel at the beginning of a word, is a semiconsonant. Thus, **Iūlius** in Latin = *Julius* in English. All of the derivatives of **iaciō** show the *j*.

A wall chart of prefixes could be produced by students for rapid review of derivatives and for use with new root verbs encountered in the course.

7. As an additional project, students may construct derivative trees to display the variety of words derived from a single Latin source. The example below may serve as a guide. Words should be arranged on the tree so that the basic derivatives are at the base of the branches (e.g., *produce* below) and the words formed from the basic derivatives come later on the same branch (e.g., *product*, *reproduce*). This project may be done by the whole class, individually, or in small groups. Students can be encouraged to bring examples of derivatives from their readings in other classes and from magazines or newspapers.

Suggested Latin words for derivative trees: **agere, cadere, capere, claudere, dūcere, labōrāre, movēre, pōnere, scrībere, sūmere,** and **venīre.** The *Latin-English Derivative Dictionary* published by the American Classical League is a useful source of derivatives; the American Classical League also offers a *Derivative Tree Chart* similar to the tree below.

Students will think of other visuals to display derivatives, e.g., a root cloud with raindrops; a school of fish with a root leader; balloons; flower petals with center root; or a hose spraying derivatives. Students' imaginations will come up with even more creative ideas.

CHAPTER 31: AT DINNER

Student's Book

1. **a.** This chapter aims to explain the use of the perfect passive participle, give practice in its use, and give further practice with the passive voice.

   b. At last, the long awaited dinner! After students have read the story and carefully noted the sequence of events at Cornelius' dinner, the teacher should invite them to compare Trimalchio's parallel but far more lavish and pretentious banquet, as it is described in the extracts from Petronius in the cultural background readings at the end of this handbook (pp. 40–42). The nearly parallel sequence of events in the two dinners may be set forth as follows:

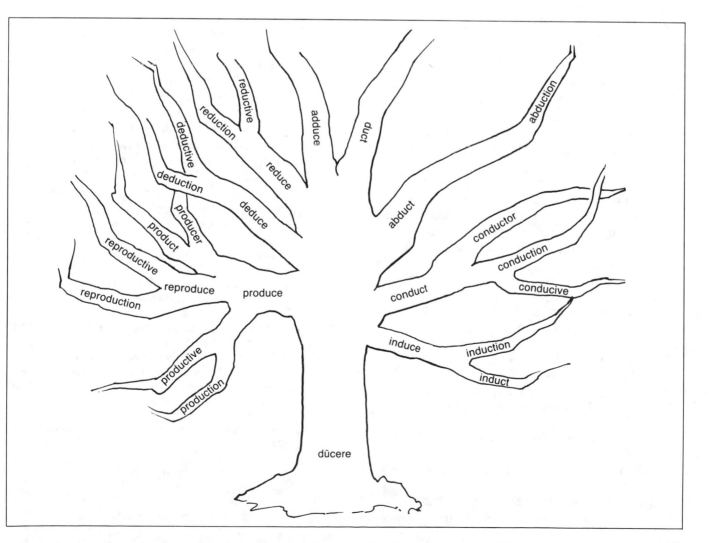

Cornelius' Dinner	Trimalchio's Banquet
Sandals are removed. (line 5)	Slaves pour ice water over hands of guests.
Guests wash hands. (line 7)	Toenails are pedicured.
Gustātiō is served. (lines 7–9)	Hors d'oeuvres are served.
Guests gossip. (lines 9–11)	Guests gossip.
Gustātiō is removed. (line 12)	Tables are wiped.
Main course is served: pork and dormice. (lines 12–14)	Episode of the three hogs; roast pork is finally brought in and and carved.
	Chef is rewarded.
Titus arrives late. (line 14)	Habinnas and wife arrive late.
Pork is carved and served. (lines 22–24)	
Pork is served to distinguished guests, scraps of chicken to **clientēs**. (lines 23–24)	[Compare Juvenal, *Satires* V on page 38 of the student's book for similar demeaning treatment of **clientēs**.]
Cook is praised. (lines 27–31)	
Tables are cleared and dessert is brought in. (lines 32–34)	Tables are removed; Trimalchio jokes over dessert; another course is served.
Wine is served. (lines 34–35)	"We'll drink until dawn!"

Careful comparison of the simple elegance of Cornelius' dinner with the ostentatious extravagance of Trimalchio's should provide opportunity for lively discussion of styles, tastes, and manners, and should also lead to discussion of the deliberately satirical purposes of Petronius as a literary artist.

This chapter also has background on Roman food, the frequent treatment of clients as "second-class citizens" at banquets of the wealthy, and an excerpt in Latin and English from Petronius.

2. The perfect passive participle is introduced without help of vocabulary notes in three sentences:

Soleae dēpositae ā servīs ablātae sunt. (5)

Itaque coquus vocātus ab omnibus laudātus est. (31)

Vīnum quoque in mēnsā positum omnibus est datum. (34–35)

These sentences may be thought of as shortened forms of compound sentences (i.e., sentences with two main clauses connected by a coordinating conjunction) such as the following:

Soleae dēpositae sunt et ā servīs ablātae sunt.

Itaque coquus vocātus est et ab omnibus laudātus est.

Vīnum quoque in mēnsā positum est et omnibus dātum est.

Or, they may be thought of as shortened forms of complex sentences (i.e., sentences with a subordinate and a main clause) such as the following:

Postquam soleae dēpositae sunt, ā servīs ablātae sunt.

Itaque ubi coquus vocātus est, ab omnibus laudātus est.

Vīnum quod in mēnsā positum est omnibus est datum.

Various translations of the original sentences with the perfect passive participles are possible depending on whether they are thought of as compound or complex sentences, and the possibilities are given and discussed on pages 34–35. Translations of any of these sorts should be accepted when the students are reading the passage at the beginning of the chapter for the first time. Students should, however, soon become aware of the *literal* translation of the perfect passive participle, and they should then be encouraged to find a translation that both makes good English and fits the context.

3. Words to be deduced: **olīva** (8), **asparagus** (9), **sē . . . excūsāre** (17–18), and **locus** (19).

4. Structures:

Interrupted sentences:

a. **Gāius, quamquam īrātissimus erat, nihil tamen dīxit. . . .** (21)

b. **Etiam clientēs, quamquam frusta modo habēbant, ūnā cum cēterīs clāmābant. . . .** (27–28)

c. **Servī, quamquam dēfessī erant, hūc illūc currēbant.** (33–34)

Note the inversion **. . . est datum. . . .** (35)

5. Notes on vocabulary and special usages:

a. **. . . Titus noster sērō venīre solet. . . .** (17): Students should always be encouraged to search for idiomatic English translations, and the verb **solēre** is particularly challenging. Teachers may wish to review some examples already met to see the variety of translations that are possible. (The translations given below are, of course, not the only ones possible.)

. . . puerī togam praetextam gerere solent. (10:3–4)

. . . are accustomed to wearing. . . .

Tabellāriī tunicās gerere solent. (15:14–15)

. . . are in the habit of wearing, normally wear. . . .

Multī viātōrēs ad meam caupōnam venīre solent. (18:11–12)

. . . habitually come. . . .

. . . multa dē aedificiīs urbis nārrāre solēbat. . . . (24:23)

. . . was inclined to. . . .

. . . Titus . . . prope arēnam sedēre solet. (26:22–23)

. . . usually sits. . . .

. . . solent esse incendia. . . . (28:15)

. . . there are regular outbreaks of fire. . . .

. . . **Titus . . . sērō venīre solet.** . . . (31:17)
   . . . generally comes late. . . .
   Gāius . . . cēnam optimam dare solet. (31:29)
   It is customary for Gaius to give. . . .

   b. Partitive genitive: **aliquid novī** (10)
   c. **medius** *middle of:* **in mediā mēnsā** (13). Cf. **medium triclīnium** (30.8).
   d. Present participle: **ambulāns** (19)
   e. **dē** in partitive sense: **dē porcō datum est** (23– 24), literally, "there was given of pork." Better English: "some pork was given."
   f. **secundās mēnsās** (32–33): It was often the custom to remove the entire table or table surface when dinner courses were changed. Thus, dessert = **secundae mēnsae**. (See the extract from Petronius on page 42 of the cultural background readings at the end of this handbook.) This was not only for the convenience of the guests but also to show off the wealth of the host, as the nobility vied for tables of ivory, inlaid marble, and precious woods. The poet Eumolpus in Petronius' *Satyricon* (119) mocks these ostentatious displays of furniture.

6. Lines 27–30 of the story provide a good passage for dictation.

7. The sentences in Exercise 31b require some changes of tense, number, and voice from the models in the story. No. 2 eliminates the perfect passive participle from the model sentence (line 5 of the story) and thus simplifies it. No. 5 expands the model sentence (line 31 in the story) into a compound sentence.

8. **Versiculī:** "Dinner Party," page 101
   a. Note that in poem *(i)* **vīnōrum** is placed early for emphasis; a more normal word-order might be: **Salvē, Tite, cūrātor nōn aquārum (sed) vīnōrum.**
   b. In poem *(ii)* dormice serve as appetizers, as at Trimalchio's banquet (see extracts in cultural background readings at the end of this handbook).

9. *Recipes and Menus:* The recipes on page 36 of the student's book are from *The Roman Cookery Book* by Apicius, translated by Barbara Flower and Elisabeth Rosenbaum (Harrap). See also *Apicius: Cookery and Dining in Imperial Rome,* a fully annotated translation of Apicius' cookbook with a full introduction. The adventurous may want to investigate *Ancient Roman Feasts and Recipes: Adapted for Modern Cooking.* Simple recipes are given in *Aspects of Roman Life Folder A,* yellow source cards 1.30 and 1.31, "Roman Recipes" (1) and (2); see also *Ten Ancient Recipes from Cato's De Agri Cultura.* For a general treatment of these topics in both Greek and Roman cultures see *Food and Drink.*

   Students may be invited to identify and describe the uses of the utensils and implements pictured at the top of page 36 of the student's book. See *Food and Drink,* "Utensils, Methods, Recipes," pp. 56–61.

   Roman banquets are always popular. The following suggestions are offered by Shirley Lowe of Wayland (Massachusetts) Junior High School:

Teachers may be encouraged to have an "authentic" Roman banquet using recipes found in the books referred to above. It could be held by a single Latin class or as a total Latin department project. It could be for students themselves or it could include invited guests (school personnel, parents, and friends). At Wayland Junior High School the Latin students are required to come in costume and to help pay for the food. Administrators and others come as spectators, and parents come and serve as helpers.

Columns, murals, a temple façade, and arches transform a cafeteria into a setting for a **cēna Rōmāna.** By arranging the tables in a giant horseshoe shape, you have a pseudotriclinium as well as a center stage area for the student-created entertainment. Latin students with musical talent provide appropriate opening music as the costumed guests parade in to their seats. After greetings from the **arbiter cēnae** and a sacrifice to Jupiter by the **sacerdōs,** the **gustātiō,** consisting of hard-cooked eggs (plain or deviled), carrot and celery sticks, black olives and cheese, is served. When the guests are not gossiping with each other, they are entertained by their classmates. With a printed program (its cover designed by a Latin student) at each place, the order of the acrobats, piano concerto, skits, commercials, singers, news broadcasts, musical groups, comics, dancers, and so forth, is easily followed. When the **gustātiō** is removed by the parent helpers, they bring out the **mēnsa** of chicken, bread, and apple and grape juice. The latter, however, is not mixed with water! Again there is a round of entertainment which this time might include toasts offered by the **arbiter bibendī.** Next there is a costume contest where participants march around the cafeteria and in front of the judges who award prizes for originality and authenticity. After the parent-**ancillae** are praised (applauded) for their assistance, the tables are cleared and the **secunda mēnsa** of cookies and apples is brought out. In this way the **cēna** concludes with the **convīvae** having had everything **ab ōvō usque ad māla.**

See also, *How to Prepare and Serve a Roman Banquet.*

The Greek "S" referred to in Martial's epigram on page 37 is the archaic Greek sigma, written C—hence the description of the couch as "crescent-shaped."

The passage from Juvenal's fifth satire on page 38 of the student's book should be read in conjunction with lines 24 and 27–30 of the story at the beginning of the chapter.

10. The reading in Latin with English translation from Petronius has been included as a counterpart to the roast pork served by Cornelius. Students should note that Cornelius' roast pork comes into the dining room complete with head; Trimalchio's does not appear even to have been gutted and

cleaned! The whole story of Trimalchio's pork is given in translation in the cultural background readings on page 41 of this handbook.

The Latin and English passages on pages 38–39 of the student's book should be handled in the same way as the passages from Pliny and Trajan at the end of Chapter 28. (See above, Chapter 28, Student's Book, note 12b.) Students should be able to make many connections between the Latin and the English translation; the sentences are simple in structure and much of the vocabulary will be familiar to students at this stage or can be easily deduced from the translation. The following words may be of special interest:

tomāculum, -ī *(n)* (diminutive of Greek *tomē*, "a cutting"): A kind of sausage (usually eaten hot and often served in **popīnae** or cook-shops).

botulus, -ī *(m)*: A black, blood pudding sausage. For recipes, see *Apicius: Cookery and Dining in Imperial Rome*, pp. 69–70.

automatum, -ī *(n)* (Greek loan word originally meaning "acting of its own will," "spontaneous," "accidental"): Trick (i.e., "something which appears to work without external agency"—as explained by M. S. Smith in his edition of Petronius, *Cena Trimalchionis*, Oxford, 1975, p. 134).

Language Activity Book

1. The activities for Chapter 31 lead the students a step further with use of the perfect passive participle in that they require the students to use participles in cases other than the nominative, to which examples were confined in the student's book. The activities thus draw out the implications of the statement on page 35 of the student's book that the perfect passive participle has the endings of an adjective of the 1st and 2nd declensions and that it must therefore agree in gender, case, and number with the noun or pronoun it modifies. Thus, in Activity 31a, students must produce the perfect passive participle of the verb given in infinitive form in parentheses and then put it in the correct gender, case, and number to modify the italicized noun.

2. Activity 31c demonstrates how a perfect passive participle may substitute for a relative clause and gives practice in converting the active constructions in the relative clauses into corresponding passive constructions with the participles. This is a challenging exercise and may require aid from the teacher.

3. In Activity 31d, note that the partitive idea in the phrase "the rest of the guests" will be translated with the adjective **cēterī** modifying the noun **convīvae**. The following is a sample translation of the paragraph:

Convīvae ad cēnam invītātī Cornēlium in ātriō exspectābant. Mox intrāvit Cornēlius et omnēs convīvās cum rīsū salūtāvit. Convīvae in triclīnium ā servīs ductī in lectīs accubuērunt. Ancillae ā Cornēliō iussae aquam portāvērunt ad convīvās quī manūs celeriter lāvērunt. Gustātiō in mēnsā posita clientēs dēlectāvit. Cēterī convīvae glīrēs ab Aurēliā ipsā ēmptōs laudāvērunt. Cēna ā Cornēliī coquō parāta ab omnibus laudāta est. Clientēs laetī erant quod eīs licēbat frustra pullōrum ad līberōs domum auferre.

REVIEW VII

Student's Book

1. The main grammatical features in Chapters 27–31 which require review are:
   a. the relative pronoun
   b. prefixes
   c. the demonstrative adjectives and pronouns: **is, ea, id; hic, haec, hoc;** and **ille, illa, illud**
   d. the present passive infinitive
   e. the forms and use of the passive voice in the present, future, imperfect, perfect, pluperfect, and future perfect tenses (agreement of the perfect passive participle with the subject of the verb)
   f. the use of the ablative case with the preposition **ā** or **ab** to designate the person by whom the action of a passive verb is performed and the use of the ablative case without a preposition to designate the thing, means, instrument, or cause.

2. Exercise VIIb may be repeated with the students substituting the correct forms of **hic, haec, hoc** and of **ille, illa, illud** instead of **is, ea, id.**

3. Exercise VIIc may also be repeated with the students substituting the correct forms of **is, ea, id.** Repetition of these exercises with the different demonstrative adjectives and pronouns can help reinforce the point that these words can be used either as pronouns (as in Exercise VIIb) or as adjectives (as in Exercises VIIc and d).

4. In Exercise VIIf, Nos. 1, 2, and 5 require the preposition.

5. Exercise VIIi contains many compound verbs. The following words are to be deduced: **abripere** (3), **respicere** (10, 15), **retrahere** (11), **remittere** (11), and **amor** (15; to be deduced from **amāre**).

Language Activity Book

Activity RVIIa; Particular care should be taken with the following points in the English to Latin translations. In No. 3, the clause "which had been fed" could be translated with a relative clause in Latin, but it is preferable to use the perfect passive participle. In No. 4, "one of the pigs" will require **ē** + *abl.*; "to Pseudolus" will be dative (indirect object); and "for six denarii" will be ablative of price without a preposition. In No. 5, the future tense must be used in both clauses. In No. 6, either the imperfect or the perfect tense could be used; the ablative without **ā** or **ab** will be used to translate "with . . ."; the word "one" is not to be translated. In Nos. 8 and 9, the future perfect passive will be used in the subordinate clauses, and in No. 9, "to the guests" requires **ad** + *acc.*

The following are sample translations of the sentences in RVIIa:

1. Ingēns onus carnis in urbe ā servīs interdiū portātum est.
2. Nihil in urbe plaustrīs interdiū portātur.
3. Porcī ā laniō pastī ad eius tabernam manū ducēbantur.
4. Ūnus ē porcīs Pseudolō ā laniō sex dēnāriīs trādētur.
5. Sī Pseudolus octō dēnāriōs dabit, ille lepus huic porcō ā laniō addētur.
6. Pseudolus hōc pinguī porcō sed nōn illō nigrō dēlectātus est.
7. Aurēlia Pseudolum pūnīrī iubēbit.
8. Ubi covīvae ā Cornēliō in ātriō cōmiter salūtātī erunt, in triclīnium dūcentur.
9. Ubi signum servīs datum erit, porcum scindent et carnem ad convīvās ferent.
10. Cornēlius ā clientibus laudātus est, quamquam frusta pullī modo eīs data sunt.

CHAPTER 32: THE COMMISSATIO

Student's Book

1. a. The comparative and superlative forms of adjectives, including the irregulars, are presented systematically. Many comparative and superlative forms have been encountered in earlier chapters.

   b. A **commissātiō** (or **comis(s)ātiō**; derived from the Greek verb *kōmazō*, "to revel," "to make merry") follows Cornelius' dinner. The traditional procedures or rituals governing the **commissātiō** are described in detail, and the outcome provides an opportunity for discussion of ancient attitudes toward social drinking and inebriation and comparison with modern views (see note 10 below).

2. For the **commissātiō**, see the references above, Chapter 29, Student's Book, note 12, and in particular *Rome: Its People, Life and Customs*, pp. 96–97. See also below, note 10. For the knucklebones (**tālī**), see *Roman Life*, pp. 244–245.

3. The story lends itself to dramatization, with students taking the parts of the narrator and of the various guests at the party.

4. Words to be deduced: **rosa** (2), **corōnāre** (3; to be deduced from **corōna** in the English introduction).

5. The following points are worthy of review or emphasis:

   a. the inverted perfect: **est allātum** (1)

   b. the principal parts of **afferō** (1) with the changes in spelling of its prefix due to assimilation (see page 11 of the student's book): **afferō, afferre, attulī, allātum**.

   c. the dative of indirect object (**omnibus convīvīs** 1) with the passive verb (**datae sunt** 1–2)

   d. **aliī . . . aliī** meaning "some . . . others" (2)

   e. the ablative of means or instrument **apiō** (2), **tālīs** (13)

   f. **et . . . et** meaning "both . . . and" (3)

   g. the pluperfect active: **biberat** (4)

   h. the partitive construction with numbers: **ūnus ē convīvīs** (5 and 17–18)

   i. the dative of possession: **cui nōmen erat Messalla** (5)

   j. the comparative adjective followed by **quam** "than": **prūdentior quam** (9)

   k. the complementary infinitive: **sinet . . . bibere** (10–11 and other examples)

   l. the partitive genitive: **nimis vīnī** (11) and **duās partēs aquae et trēs partēs vīnī** (24). The partitive genitive in these constructions may be compared with **multum vīnum** (4).

   m. the ablative of manner: **magnā vōce** and **hōc modō** (12)

   n. the irregular imperative of **ferō**: **Fer . . . !** (14)

   o. the ablative of agent with a passive verb: **Ā Gāiō . . . iactī sunt tālī.** (16–17)

   p. the ablative of manner with the preposition: **cum rīsū** (18) and **magnā cum cūrā** (20)

   q. the dative with special verbs: **mihi favet** (23)

   r. the dative of reference or advantage: **bene tibi** (25)

   s. the principal parts of **auferō** (29) with the changes of spelling of its prefix (see page 11 of the student's book): **auferō, auferre, abstulī, ablātum**

   t. the genitive after a superlative adjective: **pessimus omnium** (29–30)

   The gerund **bibendī** (6, 13, 24) should be treated as a vocabulary item at this stage; it is enough for the students to recognize the genitive case. Likewise, the deponent verb **collāpsus est** (27) should be treated as a vocabulary item.

6. Exercise 32a provides practice with translation of the perfect passive participle (see the student's book, Chapter 31, *VERBS: Perfect Passive Participles*). In No. 7, **indūcere** is to be deduced.

7. Exercise 32b provides practice in recognizing clues that indicate the need for a passive form of the verb.

8. *ADJECTIVES: Comparative and Superlative:* The introduction of comparative and superlative forms of adjectives may be facilitated with oral work in class or with simple drawings on the blackboard or overhead projector. One might, for example, make drawings of a progressively longer dog with the following captions under each picture as the beast lengthens:

   Hic canis est longus.
   Hic canis est longior quam ille.
   Hic canis est longissimus omnium.

Pieces of chalk (**crēta**), students themselves, or pictures may provide other good examples, and one can use a variety of adjectives. Students will volunteer other comparisons, and the learning of yet another bit of grammar becomes a game!

In conjunction with the list at the top of page 46,

the teacher may wish to provide further explanation of the formation of the comparative and superlative forms of adjectives.

a. The regular **-ior** and **-issimus** endings are added to the stem of the adjective, which is found by dropping the genitive singular ending (this is a good place to reinforce the concept of the stem of a noun or adjective and how it is found), e.g., ignāv*ior*, ignāv*issimus*; pulchr*ior* (for the superlative; see below); fēlīc*ior*, fē-līc*issimus*; and facil*ior* (for the superlative, see below).

b. Adjectives ending in **-er** form their superlatives irregularly by adding **-rimus** to the nominative, e.g., pulcher*rimus*.

c. Some adjectives ending in **-lis** form their superlatives irregularly by adding **-limus** to the stem (**facilis, difficilis, similis, dissimilis, gracilis,** and **humilis**), e.g., facil*limus*.

The case endings of the comparative adjectives should be compared carefully with those of 3rd declension nouns and adjectives (see Chapter 17). Note in particular that the ablative singular of comparative adjectives ends in **-e**, while that of 3rd declension adjectives ends in **-ī**.

The teacher should mention that comparative adjectives will often be followed by **quam** "than" (story, lines 9–10) and that superlatives will often be followed by a partitive genitive (story, lines 29–30) or **ex (ē)** and the ablative. The ablative of comparison without **quam** will be discussed in the next chapter; the teacher should use only the construction with **quam** in Chapter 32.

Careful note should also be taken of the other possible meanings of comparative and superlative adjectives ("rather . . . ," "too . . . ," and "very . . . ," "exceedingly . . ."), since comparatives and superlatives are often encountered without any expressed comparison.

The irregular comparatives and superlatives yield many important derivatives in English. Some of these appear in Activity 32d in the language activity book. Awareness of the English derivatives will help students learn the irregular Latin comparative and superlative adjectives.

Latin phrases used in English such as the following may also be taught at this time: a fortiori, a priori, ne plus ultra, summa cum laude, and summum bonum. The word **plūs** is given as the comparative of **multus**, but **plūs** is found only as a noun, usually with a partitive genitive.

It should be pointed out to students that **melior, peior, maior,** and **minor** are declined in the same way as **pulchrior**, which is illustrated in the chart.

9. Exercise 32e is an important reading passage. After the passage has been read and translated, the following points may be noted:

a. the adverbs in **-ē**: optimē (4), maximē (22), and celerrimē (27). Adverbs will be treated systematically in the next chapter.

b. the verb intruding between noun and adjective: **cēnam parāvit optimam** (4–5)

c. exclamatory **quam** (5), not to be confused with **quam** meaning "than"

d. **quam** used with the superlative to mean "as . . . as possible" (27)

e. the dative with compound verbs: **eī acciderat** (8) and **amīcō veterī . . . occurrerat** (9)

f. the important irregular verb **fīō** (passive of **faciō**), which is here used in the present (16), imperfect (21), and future (28) tenses (the forms of this verb will be formally presented in Chapter 44 in the fourth student's book)

g. the comparative and superlative of **ēbrius**, using **magis** and **maximē** (21–22). Compare the use of "more" and "most" in English instead of the more usual "-er" and "-est": "bigger" and "biggest," but "more beautiful" and "most beautiful." The adverbs **magis** and **maximē** are used to compare adjectives ending in **-us** proceded by *e* or *i*, such as **ēbrius, idōneus,** and **necessārius.**

10. Topics for discussion and writing in English: The cultural background readings at the end of this handbook contain selections from Plato, Xenophon, Cicero, Horace, and Seneca on the practice of drinking during the **commissātiō** following a dinner. Reading of the passages in class may be followed by discussion of each author's attitude toward drinking (advantages and disadvantages) and recommendations as to how the drinking should best proceed. Both the positive and the negative aspects of drinking as presented in the passages should be brought out in the discussion, with careful attention to what each author is saying. Then with reference to these passages and the story of the **commissātiō** after Cornelius' dinner, students could be invited to follow up the discussion with written work. There are various possibilities:

a. an essay setting forth the attitude of one of the ancient authors toward social drinking

b. a dialogue between one of the ancient authors and Cornelius on the subject of Titus' behavior

c. an essay comparing ancient and modern attitudes toward social drinking

d. a dialogue between one of the ancient authors and an officer or member of one of the SADD or MADD groups formed to combat drunken driving

Language Activity Book

1. In Activity 32b, the answer to No. 6 should be **maximē ēbrius** (cf. above, Student's Book, note 9g).

2. In Activity 32c, in Nos. 7 and 10, the perfect passive participle alone may be used to substitute for the first verb and **et** may be omitted, e.g., either:

Tālī cum fritillō ā servīs allātī sunt et in mēnsā positī sunt.

or

Tālī cum fritillō ā servīs allātī in mēnsā positī
sunt.

The latter is preferred.

CHAPTER 33: VIOLENCE IN THE STREETS

Student's Book

1. **a.** This chapter continues discussion of the use
   of comparative adjectives (constructions with
   quam and with ablative of comparison), and
   presents the formation and use of positive,
   comparative, and superlative adverbs.
   b. The banquet now over, attention shifts to a
   misfortune suffered by Eucleides. The hazards
   of urban life appear again (cf. the fire in Chapter 28), but this time as they affect a member
   of a well-to-do family. The violence suffered by
   Eucleides at the hands of thieves is matched at
   the end of the chapter by Juvenal's description
   of gratuitous violence in the streets of Rome.
   (Students will recall Marcus' dream of being attacked by thieves in Chapter 25.)
2. The positive adverb **facile** (22), the comparative
   celerius (21), and the superlatives **celerrimē** (7)
   and **fortissimē** (23), all glossed in the vocabulary
   (except for **celerrimē**, which was introduced in
   Chapter 14), pave the way for the notes on the
   formation of adverbs on pages 52–53.
3. The deponent verb **cōnsecūtī sunt** (22) should be
   treated as a vocabulary item at this stage; deponents will be discussed formally in Chapter 35.
4. Words to be deduced: **concurrere** (7) and **dēfendere** (23). Forms to be deduced: the present participles **intrantēs** (15) and **rīdentēs** (24).
5. Structures:
   Condensed sentence (with inversion of verb):
   Mihi est adēmptum baculum,
   adēmpta pecūnia. (23–24)
   Other condensed sentences occur in Exercise 33d,
   Nos. 6 and 8 (see the second teacher's handbook,
   Chapter 24, Student's Book, note 3c).
6. Notes on case usage:
   a. Dative indirect object with compound verbs:
   . . . **poētae cuidam occurrī** . . . . (11)
   . . . **ubi īnsulae iam appropinquābāmus,** . . . (14)
   b. Dative with special verbs:
   . . . **vix eī crēdidī.** (14)
   Students should be reminded of other special verbs
   they have met that take the dative case, namely,
   nocēre and **favēre**:
   Interdiū certē praedōnēs nōbīs nōn nocēbunt. (25:
   13–14)
   Ego russātīs favēbō. (26:24–25)
   c. Dative of separation:
   Mihi est adēmptum baculum, adēmpta pecūnia.
   (23–24)
   d. Partitive genitive:
   aliquid vīnī (9)
   nihil perīculī (19)

7. **Marcus Valerius Martiālis** (12): Students have already met several of Martial's epigrams in the
   second student's book, pp. 72–74, and on page 37
   of the third student's book. More epigrams by this
   keen observer of Roman life will appear in the
   fourth student's book, some of them in the original Latin. Born in Bilbilis, Spain, about A.D. 40,
   Martial went to Rome in A.D. 64, the year of the
   Great Fire, when Nero was Emperor. Soon after
   Eucleides' encounter with Martial, the poet was to
   write a collection of epigrams celebrating the dedi-
   cation by Titus of the Flavian Amphitheater or
   Colosseum (A.D. 80) (see Chapter 45 in the fourth
   student's book). For further information on Martial, see *The Oxford Classical Dictionary*, pp. 652–
   653.
8. *ADVERBS: Comparative and Superlative:* Students
   should note that **facile** (bottom of page 52 and
   Exercise 33f) is irregular in the positive. In comparing the forms of adverbs with those of adjectives
   (see suggestion at top of page 53), students will
   come to see that except for **magis** the comparative
   forms of the adverbs are identical to the neuter
   nominative/accusative singular of the comparative adjective. They should further note that the
   superlative adverbs are the same as the superlative adjectives except that they end in **-ē** (with the
   exception of **plūrimum**).
9. In exercise 33f, students may need help with the
   meaning of **longē**, "far."
10. *Juvenal on Violence in the Streets of Rome:* The issue of
    street crime in ancient Rome, with its obvious
    parallels in modern urban life, is a topic for class
    discussion and possible project work.

    The passage at the bottom of page 54 of the
    student's book is an extract from Juvenal's famous
    third satire on the dangers and indignities of living
    in Rome. As with the letters of Pliny and Trajan at
    the end of Chapter 18 and the extract from Petro-
    nius at the end of Chapter 31, teachers should
    have students read aloud first the English transla-
    tion and then the Latin. As many connections as
    possible should then be made between words and
    phrases in the Latin and in the English translation.
    Note the following vocabulary: **calx, calcis** (*f*),
    heel; **pugnus, -ī** (*m*), fist.

    A student may be asked to summarize the brief
    scene and then to elaborate it by filling in further
    details that might make it more vivid. Students
    might be asked to write an account of the episode
    suitable for publication in a newspaper. Another
    possibility is for students to locate accounts of
    similar incidents in newspapers and to compare
    them with the account in Juvenal. Discussion of
    ancient street violence, its causes, and measures
    taken against it could lead to assignment of an
    essay topic comparing violence in ancient Rome
    with street violence today. See *Daily Life in Ancient
    Rome*, pp. 47–51, and *Rome: Its People, Life and
    Customs*, pp. 37–40.

For the police protection available in the streets of Rome, see *The Oxford Classical Dictionary*, "Police," page 851. The **vigilēs** or fire brigades established by Augustus (see above, Chapter 28, Student's Book, note 12a) were of some help. Augustus also established the office of **praefectus urbī** (see *The Oxford Classical Dictionary*, p. 872) and a police force known as the **cohortēs urbānae** (see *The Oxford Classical Dictionary*, p. 258). The Pretorian Guard (**cohors praetōria**; see *The Oxford Classical Dictionary*, pp. 873–874), created by Augustus and assigned to protection of the Emperor, could intervene in extreme urban crises.

Language Activity Book

1. Activity 33a is intended to emphasize the difference between adjectives and adverbs as they are used in sentences.
2. Activity 33b gives further practice with the formation of adverbs.
3. Activity 33c contrasts the comparative construction with **quam** with the construction with the ablative.
4. In Activity 33e, students must keep in mind the meanings of the comparative and superlative other than "more" and "most." (See pages 47 and 53 of the student's book.) The following is a sample translation of the paragraph in Activity 33e:

Eucleidēs tandem domum sērissimē advēnit. Fūste maximō ferōciter percussus erat; tunica erat sordidissima et sanguine aspersa. Cornēlius tamen sollicitior erat quam Eucleidēs. "Tū gravius vulnerātus es," inquit Cornēlius, quī iussit vulnera quam celerrimē ligārī. Ubi servī Eucleidem in lectō pōnēbant, Cornēlius, hōc spectāculō magnopere affectus, "Dīligentius," inquit, "eum movēte!" Deinde Cornēlius trīstissimē Eucleidī, "Fortissimus," inquit, "certē fuistī, Eucleidēs. Praedōnēs illī, cum inventī erunt, vehementissimē pūnientur."

WORD STUDY IX

1. The aims of this section are:
   a. to explain the formation of Latin adjectives with the suffixes **-ōsus**, **-idus**, and **-bilis**
   b. to present the English derivatives of such adjectives
   c. to give examples of Latin words and expressions in current use in the legal profession
2. Latin adjectives in **-ōsus** are not the only source of English words ending in *-ous*. Latin adjectives ending in **-ius**, **-eus**, and **-uus** may also become English words which end in *-ous*, e.g., **strēnuus**, *strenuous*; **dubius**, *dubious*; **igneus**, *igneous*.
3. In Exercise 2, students should be advised that there is no English derivative from **madidus** (No. 10).

4. Students should learn the anglicized pronunciation of the Latin legal terms in Exercise 4, contrasting it with their own classical pronunciation. For some of the terms the difference in the two pronunciations will be relatively slight, as in the case of *nolo contendere*. For those with markedly different pronunciations, the following guide will be useful:

prima facie (prī' mə fā' shē)	delicti (de lik' tī)
subpoena (sə pē' nə)	fide (fīd *or* fī' dē)
habeas (hā' bē əs)	jure (joor' e)

5. For more information on Latin in the law, see a legal dictionary such as *Black's Law Dictionary*. An instructional unit on legal Latin is provided in *Legal Latin: Teacher's Guide*. *Legal Terms* is a useful chart to display while this section is being taught. For a comprehensive study of Roman law and legal practice, one may consult *Law and Life of Rome*.
6. Teachers are encouraged to keep a file of clippings from magazines and newspapers of Latin legal phrases. Seeing such phrases in use is a great incentive for learning them.

Individual students could be assigned one of the phrases in Exercise 5 and asked to be on the lookout in newspapers and magazines for examples or illustrations of these legal maxims today. This could be a month-long assignment, and at the end of the given time information could be presented to the class orally and visually.

Students could also be encouraged to interview local lawyers for precedent-setting cases which illustrate the maxims in Exercise 5 or are examples of the phrases in Exercise 4.

CHAPTER 34: A LETTER

Student's Book

1. a. This chapter provides examples and discussion of the Roman method of giving dates.
   b. Five more deponent verbs are used in the story and given in the vocabulary: **morātus est** (7), **regressus est** (7), **proficīscētur** (8), **secūtī sunt** (20), and **cōnātus est** (20) (**cōnsecūtī sunt**, which appears in line 21 has already been encountered in the previous chapter). Full discussion of deponent verbs will be found in the next chapter.
   c. Cornelia's letter to Flavia tells of the fire and of Eucleides's recent encounter with the robbers, thus recapping these themes of the hazards of life in the city. Coincidentally, the day before Cornelia wrote this letter her father received a letter from a certain Valerius, who is introduced here and who will become increasingly important for Cornelia as the stories progress. The letter in this chapter is pivotal, looking

both backward to Cornelia's childhood friend and forward to her husband.

Cultural material at the end of this chapter introduces the theme of Roman education, which will be developed in Chapters 35 to 38, focusing on the boys, Marcus and Sextus. There is further, supplementary material on Roman education in the cultural background readings at the end of this handbook, some of which should be used in conjunction with the extracts at the end of the present chapter. With Chapters 39 and 40 the story will return to Cornelia and Valerius.

2. Word to be deduced: **vulnerāre** (23).

3. The various dates are given in the vocabulary list and may be explained when dealing with the note on Dates (pages 59–60). Let this explanation follow comprehension of the content of the letter.

4. Student's attention should be called to the place clues, which will be treated formally in Chapter 37:

Brundisiī (4) "at Brundisium"
Rōmam (5, 8, 11, and 26) "to Rome"
in Bīthȳniā (7) "in Bithynia"
in Italiam (7) "into Italy"
Brundisium (7) "to Brundisium"
Brundisiō (8) "from Brundisium"

The context of each sentence, the general sense of the passage, and in particular the verbs within each sentence provide clues to the meaning of the place expressions (and students should be taught to pay attention to each of these clues), but it is not too early to point out that the accusative indicates place to which, the ablative expresses place from which, and a form that looks like the genitive singular shows place where (all with names of cities: contrast **in Bīthȳniā**, line 7).

5. The ablative of degree of difference with a comparative adverb appears for the first time in line 10: **multō libentius**.

6. Structures:
   a. Interrupted sentences:
      . . . **Eucleidēs noster, ab urbe domum rediēns, duōs hominēs . . . exeuntēs vīdit.** (18–19)
      Quī hominēs, ubi Eucleidem cōnspexērunt, statim eum secūtī sunt. (19–20)
   b. Linking **quī: Quī hominēs. . . .** (19)
   c. Balance:
      Quō celerius currēbat ille,
      eō celerius currēbant hominēs. (20–21)

7. This is a useful passage to illustrate how pieces of information pertaining to a noun and its participle are often placed between the noun and the participle, e.g.:
   a. **Haec** *epistula* **ā Valeriō prīdiē Īdūs Octōbrēs** *scrīpta* **Rōmam post vīgintī diēs advēnit!** (4–5)
      The words between **epistula** and **scrīpta** tell us by whom and when the letter was written,

wheras **Rōmam post vīgintī diēs** tells us where and when the letter arrived.
   b. . . . *Eucleidēs noster,* **ab urbe domum** *rediēns,* **duōs** *hominēs* **ē popīnā quādam** *exeuntēs* **vīdit.** (18–19)
      In this example, the words **ab urbe domum** go closely with **Eucleidēs . . . rediēns**, whereas the words **ē popīnā quādam** go with **hominēs . . . exeuntēs**.

Compare the following arrangement:
      Ā praedōnibus correptus ac fūstibus percussus, gravissimē vulnerātus est. (22–23)
      In this example, the phrase **ā praedōnibus** goes with **correptus; fūstibus** goes with **percussus;** and **gravissimē** goes with **vulnerātus est**.

If students are trained to analyze phrases, clauses, and sentences in this way when dealing with simple examples, they will find less difficulty in handling complicated Latin periods.

8. Vocabulary: it should be emphasized that different translations are often necessary for the perfect tense, e.g., **morātus est** (7) "he has stayed," but **secūtī sunt** (20) "they followed."

9. Besides commenting on the form of the Roman letter, teachers may wish to discuss the Roman postal system. The system for conveying the Emperor's mail has already been alluded to in the first student's book where the Cornelii had the unfortunate encounter with the **tabellārius** (Chapter 13) and in "Eavesdropping" in the second student's book (pages 39–40; see page 18, note 8 of the second teacher's handbook for background reading on the **cursus pūblicus**). The delivery of letters between private individuals was a much more haphazard affair. If it was known that someone was to be traveling to another part of the country, or even abroad, it was common for friends to entrust the person with mail for friends or associates in that place or along the route.

For more information on correspondence between private individuals, see *Roman Life*, "Travel and Correspondence," pp. 304–313 (excellent illustrations).

10. *Dates:*
   a. The old rhyme goes
      "In March, July, October, May, the Nones fall on the 7th day.
      In March, July, October, May, the Ides fall on the 15th day."
      Another version goes
      "March, July, October, May,
      Have Nones the 7th and Ides the 15th day."
   b. Students should note that **Iānuārius, Februārius**, etc., are adjectives agreeing with **Kalendae, Nōnae,** and **Īdūs**.

      Students may deduce the names of the twelve months from Exercise 34b (see also exercise 36b), or teachers may give them the names. Students will also want to know what the names mean in Latin; some they can deduce, others the teacher may give. The names of the months as follows are all adjectives, with which one may supply the word **mēnsis** (*m*), "month." The etymologies that follow the name of each month are taken from the *Oxford Latin Dictionary*:

Iānuārius, -a, -um (named after Janus, the god of gates and doorways)

Februārius, -a, -um (from **februa, -ōrum,** *n pl*, purificatory offerings)

Martius, -a, -um (named after Mars, the god of war)

Aprīlis, -is, -e (meaning unknown; perhaps Etruscan in origin. Varro, writing about the Latin language in the 1st century B.C., and suggesting an etymology now generally regarded as false, commented, . . . **putō dictum, quod vēr omnia aperit,** *De lingua Latina* VI.33)

Māius, -a, -um (perhaps derived from the name of an old deity, **Māius,** related etymologically to the adjective **magnus**)

Iūnius, -a, -um (named after Juno, wife of Jupiter and queen of the gods)

Iūlius, -a, -um (named after Julius Caesar; previously this month was named **Quīntīlis, -is, -e**)

Augustus, -a, -um (named after Augustus, the first Roman emperor; previously this month was named **Sextīlis, -is, -e**)

September, -bris, -bre (the seventh, later the ninth, month)

Octōber, -bris, -bre (the eighth, later the tenth, month)

November, -bris, -bre (the ninth, later the eleventh, month)

December, -bris, -bre (the tenth, later the twelfth, month)

c. Students will be interested to know that our ninth, tenth, eleventh, and twelfth months were once the seventh, eighth, ninth, and tenth Roman months, because the Roman year formerly started in March. In doing Activity 36e of the language activity book, students are sent to the encyclopedia to find out more about changes made in the calendar. This activity takes its place along with other work with ordinal numerals in Chapter 36.

d. In converting years designated according to Christian reckoning to the Roman system, one subtracts from 754 (not 753) because of the Roman inclusive system of counting (compare the counting of days back from the "special days," in which the "special day" itself is counted).

e. Teachers wishing more information on the Roman calendar will find a brief account in *The Oxford Classical Dictionary*, "Calendars," pp. 192–193, and a full and detailed treatment in *The Roman Origin of Our Calendar*. See also, *Encyclopaedia Britannica*, "Calendar."

   Calendars with the dates in Latin are available each year from the American Classical League (see Bibliography). They are inexpensive additions to the overall ambience of the Latin classroom and provide excellent reinforcement for this chapter. Teachers may prefer to have students make their own calendars for given months with all the dates filled in. This could result in a colorful poster project for all students to enjoy and learn from. Each month of the school year could be done with significant dates highlighted. Older students might even want to check into the dates of some Roman holidays (**fastī**) to record on the room calendar.

11. Exercise 34c: In addition to students giving their own birthday in Latin, they might be asked from this chapter on to write the date in Latin on all papers turned in. This would provide continued reinforcement with little effort.

12. Versiculī: "Hydra Lernaeus," page 102

   a. Words to be deduced: **dēnsa** (1), **serpentīna** (5), **fīxa** (6), **duplex** (8), **decimum** (10), **hydra** (10), **hērōs** (11), **exstincta** (13; from **exstinguere** in Chapter 28), and **flammantem** (14).

   b. **perīclum** (19) = **perīculum**

   c. Content and grammar questions:
      Who speaks lines 1–2?
      What case are the words **arboribus magnīs** (3) and why?
      Mention six things about the hydra as it is described in lines 4–6.
      What use of the ablative is represented in the words **summīs . . . vīribus** (7)? What preposition could have been used with these words?
      What tense is each of the following verbs? **oppugnat** (9), **minuit** (9), **trūserat** (10), **fuerant** (11), **dēstruxerat** (11), and **videt** (12)
      What feeling on the part of Hercules is suggested in the words **Quid faceret?** (13)?
      What new measures does Hercules take (13–16)?
      Why can't Hercules overcome the last head?

   d. Matters of style: The following activities and questions may be assigned to students; some possible answers are given in brackets.
      Locate an effective example of alliteration. [line 2]
      Why is the phrase **quaterna quater** (6) more effective than the simple word **sēdecim**?
      What two words are especially carefully placed in lines 7 and 8? [**ūnī** and **duplex**]
      Locate a word used three times in three different cases within the space of two lines. [**fūstem, fūstibus, fūste,** 8–9] This is the rhetorical figure known as polyptoton, the employment of the same word in various cases. Locate two examples of anaphora. [11–12 and 19]
      Locate an example of apostrophe, in which the poet "addresses" Hercules. [19]
      What word occurs in both the first and last lines of the poem? [**ingentis/ingentī**] How does this repetition comment on Hercules' achievement?

   e. As a final question for discussion or a written essay, students might be asked to what extent

Hercules' ultimate success is dependent on (1) the advice of Minerva, (2) his own strength, and (3) his own ingenuity.

13. *Roman Education I:* The following brief notes on people mentioned in the selections from ancient authors may aid in discussion of these passages:

a. On Tacitus, *Dialogus* 28: Cornelia was a daughter of Scipio Africanus and married Tiberius Sempronius Gracchus. She had twelve children, but only three survived infancy and childhood: Sempronia, Tiberius Gracchus, and Gaius Gracchus. After her husband's death in 154 B.C., she devoted herself to the upbringing of her children. Her two sons took up agrarian reform and other radical measures that led ultimately to their deaths (in 133 and 121 B.C., respectively). Cornelia was an unusual woman and tried to influence her sons' stormy political careers. Extracts of one of her letters (much admired by Cicero) survive.

Aurelia, the mother of Julius Caesar, kept close watch on him and his wife Pompeia.

Augustus, born in 63 B.C. and originally named C. Octavius, was brought up by his mother Atia after his father died in 59 B.C.

b. On Pliny, *Letters* IV.13: Pliny the Younger (ca. A.D. 61–ca. 112) offered to give one-third of the money it would take to hire teachers to come to Comum, his native town in northern Italy, to set up a school there so that the native sons would not have to go elsewhere (such as to **Mediolānum**, Milan) for their education.

c. On Plutarch, *Cato the Elder* 20: Marcus Porcius Cato Censorius (243–149 B.C.) was a conservative opponent of the Hellenizing influences of his day and was famous for the severity of his censorship in 184. He wrote a treatise on agriculture (*De agricultura*) and a history of Italy (*Origines*). Plutarch also mentions that he wrote histories in large letters so that his son could learn about the famous men of the past without leaving the house.

d. On Plutarch, *Aemilius Paulus* 6: Lucius Aemilius Paulus Macedonicus (consul 182 and 168 B.C., died 160 B.C.) brought an end to the Third Macedonian War with victory at Pydna. He represented a blend of traditional Roman values with Hellenic culture. Plutarch emphasizes his unusual personal interest in the education of his sons.

e. On Libanius, *Orations* 58.8: Libanius was a Greek rhetorician of the fourth century A.D. For **paedagōgī**, see *Roman Life,* p. 151 (with illustrations). Horace's father served as **paedagōgus** to his son (*Satires* I.6.81–84) and carefully sheltered him in the great city of Rome to which he took him for his education.

14. For further background on Roman education, see the following:

a. *Rome: Its People, Life and Customs,* "Education," pp. 167–173.

b. *Roman Life,* "Education," pp. 148–157.

c. *Daily Life in Ancient Rome,* "Education and Religion," pp. 101–121.

d. *These Were the Romans,* "Growing Up," pp. 77–81.

e. *Education in Ancient Rome:* for education in the home during the earliest years, see Chapters II and III, "Education within the Family: (I) Parents and Relatives, (II) Private Tutors from Distant Lands," pp. 10–33; for the primary school, see Chapter IV, "Primary Schools and 'Pedagogues'," pp. 34–46, and Chapter XIII, "Primary Education: Reading, Writing, and Reckoning," pp. 165–188.

In the cultural background readings at the end of this handbook will be found extracts from Quintilian's treatise on education.

Language Activity Book

Activity 34a is an exercise in Latin composition and creative writing. Students should be encouraged to consult the previous stories for vocabulary and constructions and should be urged and warned to limit their writing to the kinds of things that have been said in Latin in the stories and variations on them. Discipline as well as creativity is required in this kind of exercise. The English translation will serve as a check on the Latin.

CHAPTER 35: OFF TO SCHOOL

Student's Book

1. a. This chapter explains deponent verbs and reviews the various uses of **quam**.

b. By way of the readings on the two earliest stages of Roman education (education in the home and education at the primary school) at the end of Chapter 34, we pass from Cornelia to the boys Marcus and Sextus as typical Roman schoolboys attending the secondary school (the third stage of Roman education) conducted by a **grammaticus** named Palaemon. This chapter begins to suggest the rigors of the life of a Roman schoolboy and typical attitudes toward school. The chapter concludes with a verbatim presentation of expressions actually used in ancient Roman classrooms.

2. Words to be deduced: **lanterna** (15) and **praeferre** (15)

Idiom to be deduced: **memoriā tenēre** "to remember" (5)

Grammar to be deduced: new compound verb with dative, . . . **eīs praeferēbat** . . . . "carried it in front of them" (15)

3. Structures:

List: . . . **invītī ē lectō surrēxērunt, vestēs induērunt, iēntāculum celerrimē sumpsērunt.** (13–14)

4. The adverb **cotīdiē** (3) may be contrasted with the phrase **in diēs** (Exercise 32e, line 16). By comparing contexts, students will discover that **cotīdiē**

refers to daily repetition, whereas **in diēs** refers to a cumulative process. Students will need to make this distinction in the language activity book, Activity 35c, Nos. 2 and 3.

5. The lantern mentioned in line 15 of the story illustrates the fact that school began very early in the morning, as can be seen by the passage from Martial quoted on page 62 of the student's book. An interesting description of the morning routine of a schoolboy living in the third century A.D. may be found in *Roman Family Life*, p. 29.

6. Line 5 marks the first mention of Vergil in the stories. At this point, however, teachers need give only a brief identification of Vergil and his place in Latin literature. Further discussion may be left until Chapters 36 and 37, where Vergil is taken up more fully.

   At this point particular mention should be made of the role of rote memory in Roman schooling (**versūs Vergiliī memoriā tenēre**, 5). Students were required to commit to memory extensive passages from both Greek and Roman literature, reference to which was supposed to aid them in their attitudes and decisions in later life. In a world where few people were able to read and the art of oratory was supreme, training of the memory was essential, as was implied in the maxim **memoria est thēsaurus omnium rērum et custōs**.

7. Sextus' thoughts (lines 3–8) make excellent material for dictation, since they include a number of new deponent verbs.

8. *Deponent Verbs:* Students are often confused by the concept of deponent verbs, since there is no parallel in English which might help their understanding. Indeed, although clearly related to the middle voice in Greek, in which the subject is thought of as acting upon or for itself, deponents are largely unique to Latin.

   It should be impressed upon students that, apart from the imperative, there are no new forms to be learned, but rather a new use of passive forms already learned. Students should be directed back to the original presentation and charts of the passive forms in Chapters 28 and 30. We do not print full sets of forms for the deponent verbs because we believe that students should learn that the forms are identical to the passive forms they have already learned. A useful classroom exercise consists of constructing charts of forms of deponent verbs on the board, with the students using the passive forms in Chapters 28 and 30 as references.

   The primary challenge of deponents is one of vocabulary-learning and of knowing whether a given verb is deponent or not. Knowing the principal parts is essential (the list of verbs on page 65, arranged by conjugation, should be learned thoroughly). This is the key to distinguishing the passive meaning of, for example, **audīminī** "you are heard" from the active meaning of **experīminī** "you test."

   The infinitives of deponent verbs should be compared with what the students have already learned about the passive infinitives of nondeponent verbs (page 21 of the student's book). Again, it should be emphasized that there is really nothing new to learn here.

   The imperative forms of deponent verbs are identical to the passive imperatives of nondeponent verbs, which are rarely used and are not taught in this course (e.g., **Amāre! Amāminī!** "Be loved!"). The imperatives of deponent verbs of course have active meanings, and they are presented on pages 64–65 of the student's book and should be learned. In the singular these imperative forms are the same as what would be the present active infinitive if deponent verbs had a present active infinitive, e.g., **Cōnāre!** and **Verēre!** Or, another way of describing these forms is to say that they are identical to an alternate 2nd person singular passive indicative form, e.g., **amāre** (= **amāris**) "you are loved." In the plural the forms are the same as the 2nd person plural of the indicative, e.g., **Cōnāminī!** and **Verēminī!**

   In connection with paragraph number 4 at the top of page 65, it should be pointed out to students that prior to the introduction of deponent verbs they could not say "having done something" in Latin, since nondeponent verbs have only a perfect *passive* participle. Deponent verbs, which have perfect participles that are passive in form but *active* in meaning, will now provide a way of saying "having done something," as is illustrated in the sample sentence in this paragraph of the student's book.

9. In Exercise 35c, No. 10, **colloquī** is to be deduced.

10. The **sententiae** in this chapter (page 66) were chosen primarily as illustrations of deponent verbs, but they also provide illustration of a comparative adjective (**meliōra**) and the substantive use of adjectives (**multī, paucī,** and **pauca**).

11. *Roman Education II:* This excerpt from a Latin phrase book for foreign students offers an interesting parallel with the modern world, in which there are so many migrant people struggling to learn new languages in order to be assimilated into their new communities. The source is the *Corpus glossariorum latinorum III.*

   As a related project, the teacher might ask students to create a book of school-related phrases in Latin, for use by an imaginary Roman child who suddenly finds himself in a 20th century classroom. Phrases could take the form of school rules, e.g.:

Nōlīte currere per andrōnēs! *No running in the halls!*

Cōnficite pēnsum! *Do your homework!*

or popular expressions, e.g.:

Nīl permovēminī! *Be cool!*
Nīl sūdōris! *No sweat!*

For additional projects on Roman education which are based on Roman sources, see *Roman Family Life*, p. 35, and the accompanying *Aspects of Roman Life Folder A* (white card 5.12, "Growing up and going to school," and yellow source cards 1.24 and 1.25, of the same title).

Language Activity Book

1. In Activity 35c, No. 2, **cotīdiē** is the Latin equivalent of the cue, "every day." In No. 3, the Latin for "day by day" is **in diēs**. See above, Student's Book, note 4. Although the participle to be supplied in Activity 35c, No. 11, could be made to modify **praedōnēs**, the events of story 33 suggest that the participle should be made to modify **Eucleidem**. The English expression, "having left," requires a deponent verb in Latin. In Activity 35c, No. 14, **puerīs** is dative with the compound verb **praeferre**. See above, Student's Book, note 2.

2. In Activity 35d, students should be encouraged to translate "But Sextus replied to him" with linking **quī: Cui tamen Sextus respondit**. The following is a sample translation of the English paragraph:

Puerī ante lūcem profectī Eucleidem ad lūdum invītī sequēbantur. Mox tamen praeteriērunt paedagōgum veterem quī strēnuissimē eōs cōnsequī cōnābātur. Palaemon, grammaticus ille ērudītissimus, ad iānuam lūdī morābātur. Puerī in lūdum ingredī nōn veritī sunt quod Palaemon eōs cōmius salūtāvit. Marcus in lūdum ingressus Sextō, "Quam cōmiter," inquit, "hic grammaticus nōs accipit!" Sextus eī, "Paulīsper," respondit, "morāre, Marce. Nōndum ille nōs expertus est."

REVIEW VIII

Student's Book

1. The main grammatical features in Chapters 32–35 that require review are:
   a. regular and irregular comparative and superlative forms of adjectives and adverbs and their uses in sentences
   b. deponent verbs
   c. four different uses of **quam**
   Some teachers will want to include review of the Roman method of giving dates.
2. Exercise VIIIa gives practice with the comparatives and superlatives, requiring students to produce the correct forms. In No. 10, **tabernārius** is to be deduced.
3. Exercises VIIIb and c give practice with the depo-

nent verbs; Exercise VIIIb requires a knowledge of principal parts.
4. Exercises VIIId and e are parallel exercises with active verbs and are included to provide review of the active forms along with the passive forms of the deponent verbs.
5. Exercise VIIIg has many deponent and passive verb forms. **Trōia** (1) and **Trōiānī** (2, 6, 7, and 14) are to be deduced.
6. In Exercise VIIIh students are required to be able to distinguish between passive forms of regular verbs and deponent verbs. Students *must* know which verbs are deponent.

Language Activity Book

Activity RVIIIa: In No. 1, students could write **prūdentior Gāiō** or **prūdentior quam Gāius**. In No. 2, "collapsed and was carried" is best translated with a deponent perfect participle followed by the perfect passive indicative. In No. 4, "as . . . as possible" should be **quam** + the superlative adverb. In No. 5, "in a few days" should be ablative of time without a preposition. The expression in No. 6 ("How happy Cornelia will be . . . !") needs to be transformed into an adverbial expression in Latin: **Quam libenter . . . vidēbit!** This may be difficult for some students, but students should always be urged to look back to the stories for vocabulary, idiom, and expression when translating from English to Latin. Usually they will find in the stories what they need to handle the English to Latin translations. No. 7 is a future more vivid construction, requiring the future tense in both clauses in Latin. In No. 8, "before dawn" in Latin would be "before the light (of day)." In No. 9, "remember" is to be translated with the Latin idiom **memoriā tenēre**. In No. 10, "very many useful things" requires the connective **et** between the two adjectives in Latin: **plūrima et ūtilia**.

The following are sample translations of the sentences in RVIIIa:

1. Nēmō est arbiter bibendī prūdentior Gāiō. Aquam et vīnum miscet prūdentius quam omnēs aliī.
2. Titus, quī nimis vīnī bibit, subitō collāpsus ē triclīniō quam celerrimē lātus est.
3. Eucleidēs, ubi duo hominēs quī fūstēs ferēbant ē popīnā sē praecipitāvērunt, celerius ambulāre cōnātus est.
4. Eucleidēs, timōre affectus, domum quam brevissimō tempore regressus est.
5. Valerius Brundisiō domum paucīs diēbus adveniet.
6. Quam libenter Cornēlia eum vidēbit!
7. Ea etiam laetior erit ubi Flāviam vidēbit.
8. Marcō et Sextō ad lūdum ante lūcem proficīscī necesse est.
9. Sextus autem domī manēre vult quod versūs Vergiliī memoriā tenēre nōn potest.

10. Palaemon, grammaticus ērūdītior, puerōs plūrima et ūtilia docēre cōnābitur.

CHAPTER 36: THE LESSONS BEGIN

Student's Book

1. a. There are no major new grammatical points in this story.

   b. We know from Sextus' complaint in Chapter 35 (line 5) that the students have been studying Vergil, as was usual in Roman schools at this level. Chapter 36 opens with a student recounting the adventures of Aeneas as told by Vergil to the point of his arrival in Carthage and his narration of his wanderings to Dido. The classroom dialogue concludes with Marcus reciting the first lines of the second book of the *Aeneid*. A background note in English (pp. 74–75 of the student's book) briefly recounts the adventures of Aeneas after leaving Dido, his founding of Lavinium, his son's founding of Alba Longa, and the founding of Rome by Romulus and Remus. This provides background for a Latin reading on the seven kings of Rome. The chapter ends as did the previous chapter with a snatch of Latin dialogue from an ancient classroom, this time showing how a Roman **grammaticus** would teach the first line of the second book of the *Aeneid*.

2. Words to be deduced: **Trōia** (4), **Asia** (6), **Hesperia** (7) (the teacher may have to explain "the land in the West," i.e., to the west of Greece; cf. the cognate **vesper**, *m*, or **vespera, -ae**, *f*, "the evening," "the west"; all of these words are from a single Greek root *wesp-* meaning "western" or "evening"), **Sicilia** (8), **tempestās** (9), **Āfrica** (9), **Trōiānus** (15), and **respōnsum** (17).

3. Various minor points of grammar:

   a. Note the phrase **quis ē vōbīs** (2), using the preposition with the ablative instead of a partitive genitive (cf. the familiar **ūnus ē discipulīs** in line 4). The genitive of the personal pronouns is not used in a partitive sense.

   b. **decem annōs** (4): accusative of duration of time, indicating "how long."

   c. The stock phrase **terrā marīque** (7–8) shows an ablative of place where without a preposition. For the ablative singular of 3rd declension neuter i-stems, see the second teacher's handbook, Chapter 17, Student's Book, note 13.

   d. **alter discipulus** (14): here "the *next* pupil."

   e. Note linking **quī** (17) = "and he."

   f. Almost everything in the passage from Vergil (*Aeneid* II.1–3) can be deduced from the translation, but it should be pointed out that **conticuēre** = **conticuērunt** (3rd person plural, perfect active) "they fell silent." **ōra:** literally, "mouths," here = "faces," "expressions." **orsus est:** from the deponent verb **ordior, ordīrī** (4), **orsus sum**, "to begin."

4. Structures:

   a. Condensed phrase: . . . **capta et incēnsa est**. (5)

   b. List: . . . **dē urbe Trōiā, dē rēbus Trōiānīs, dē perīculīs itineris**. (14–15)

5. The sentence beginning **Aenēās ipse**. . . . (9) is longer than most of the sentences that the students have encountered. It is not complicated, but it will be important that the students tackle it phrase by phrase as it unfolds. The word **cum** may cause a momentary problem. Does it mean "when" or "with"? The students must leave the decision until they have examined the rest of the sentence.

6. For a brief account of the wanderings of Aeneas from Troy to Carthage (*Aeneid* III), see *Mythology*, pp. 320–328. This version of the story by Edith Hamilton is very suitable for reading aloud to students in class.

7. Exercise 36a: The sentences in this exercise require more manipulation of the Latin in the story than is usual in this kind of exercise, and they might appropriately be assigned as written work, to be done either in class or as homework. If done as written work in class, pairs or teams of students might be asked to work on the sentences together.

8. *Numbers in Latin:* This note continues the presentation of numbers begun in Chapter 15 and Word Study IV, which may usefully be reviewed at this time.

   The terms *cardinal* and *ordinal* may not be familiar to students. The former, meaning "principal," is derived from the Latin noun **cardō, cardinis** *(m)*, "hinge," "pivot," "critical juncture," "pivotal point." Ordinal numbers, in keeping with the derivation of the word from the Latin noun **ordō, ordinis** *(m)*, "order," indicate sequence or order.

9. *The Legend of the Foundation of Rome:* Further pages from Edith Hamilton's *Mythology* (pp. 328–342) may be read to the students to complete the story of Aeneas as told in the *Aeneid*.

   In dealing with the quotation from the first book of the *Aeneid* on page 75, teachers should remind students that they have seen the word **mēta**, "mark," "goal," "turning-post," in the context of chariot racing in Chapter 26 of the second student's book.

10. In Exercise 36d, note the condensed phrase **capta et dēlēta est** (8), the ablative **Tiberī** (9), and the omission of **est** after **factus** (9). Words to be deduced: **templum** (5), **ferōcitās** (7), **Iovis Capitōlīnī** (10), **ultimus** (15), and **natūra** (16). The form **dīs** (3, 4) is more common than **deīs**; likewise, the nominative and vocative plurals are commonly written **dī**, e.g., **Dī immortālēs!** (33:5–6). The traditional dates of the kings of Rome are as follows:

   Romulus: 753–716 B.C.

Numa: 715–673 B.C.
Tullus Hostilius: 673–642 B.C.
Ancus Martius: 642–617 B.C.
Tarquinius Priscus: 616–579 B.C.
Servius Tullius: 578–535 B.C.
Tarquinius Superbus: 534–510 B.C.

The teacher may wish to reinforce the reading in Exercise 36d with pictures or slides and stories from the first book of Livy's history.

Pictures: Huts on the Palatine Hill like the **casa Romulī**: *Pictorial Dictionary of Ancient Rome*, Vol. I, pp. 163–165. See *Rome and Environs*, p. 125, for early settlement on the Palatine. The **Rēgia**, home of Numa Pompilius and later of the **Pontificēs Maximī**, situated at the east end of the **Forum Rōmānum** (the present remains date from a rebuilding in 36 B.C.: *Pictorial Dictionary of Ancient Rome*, Vol. I, pp. 264–267. See also *Rome and Environs*, p. 122.
The **Pōns Sublicius** (sublicius, -a, -um, "supported on wooden props"; this bridge was famed as the site of Horatius Cocles's stand against the attack of the Etruscans led by Porsenna: Livy II.10): no remains of the ancient bridge are visible, but it was located where the Ponte Aventino now stands. See *Rome and Environs*, p. 92.
The **Templum Iovis Capitōlīnī**: *Pictorial Dictionary of Ancient Rome*, Vol. I, pp. 530–533. See *Rome and Environs*, pp. 55–56.

Stories: The death and deification of Romulus: Livy I.16.
Numa's achievements: Livy I.19.
The war with Alba Longa: Livy I.22–29 (the famous battle of the Horatii and the Curiatii took place during this war: Livy I.24–26).
The rape of Lucretia, expulsion of Tarquinius Superbus, and creation of the first consuls: Livy I.57–60.
See also, *Myths of the Greeks and Romans*, "The Quest for a Roman Past," pp. 349–372, for more on these legends and tales of early Roman history.

11. *Roman Education III:* For more information about the secondary school and the **grammaticus**, see the references above in Chapter 34, Student's Book, note 13. For a detailed treatment, see *Education in Ancient Rome*, Chapter V, "Schools of Grammar and Literature," pp. 47–64, and Chapters XIV and XV, "The Grammatical Syllabus (I) The Elements of Metre and the Parts of Speech and (II) Correctness in Speech and Writing," pp. 189–211, and Chapters XVI and XVII, "Study of the Poets: (I) Reading Aloud and Reciting and (II) From Reading to Commentary," pp. 212–249. See also the extracts from Quintilian at the end of this handbook, pp. 44–46.

The grammarian Priscian (**Prisciānus**) was born at Caesarea in Mauretania (northwest Africa) and taught in Constantinople in the 6th century A.D. He wrote the *Institutiones grammaticae*, an eighteen volume work on Latin grammar that treats the parts of speech and syntax. The passage quoted here is from his *Partitiones XII versuum Aeneidos*.

Topics for Discussion and Writing:

The question of the extent to which girls and young women had access to education in the Roman world has been much debated. Bonner cites the evidence from primary sources on pages 27–28, 107, and 135–136 of *Education in Ancient Rome*. The teacher may summarize this evidence for the students or assign one or two students to read these pages and summarize the evidence for the class. Possible topics for discussion and essays in English include the following:

a. Why was access to education for girls and young women limited in Roman society?

b. What were the advantages and disadvantages to Roman society of limiting access to education for girls and young women?

c. In what countries today is access to education for girls (as opposed to education for boys) severely limited? Why do such limits exist?

d. What limitations, if any, are there in North America today to access to education for girls and young women?

e. What differences between modern North American and ancient Roman society can be attributed to the more open access to education for girls and young women in the former?

Language Activity Book

1. Activities 36b and c are based on Exercise 36d in the student's book.

2. Activities 36d and e develop from Exercise 36b, Nos. 6 and 7 in the student's book. For a full account of the Roman calendar, see *The Roman Origins of Our Calendar*. The *Encyclopaedia Britannica* is a convenient reference for Activity 36e.

CHAPTER 37: A LESSON FOR SEXTUS

Student's Book

1. a. This chapter teaches expressions of time and place.

   b. Palaemon continues the lesson begun in the previous chapter with a series of questions on the first line of the second book of the *Aeneid* and the wanderings of Aeneas in the manner of Priscian as seen at the end of the previous chapter. As could be expected from Sextus' attitude toward school, he gets into trouble and is disciplined. Readings later in the chapter focus on the *Aeneid* as part of an epic tradition and on the life of Vergil. The chapter concludes with a glimpse of higher education provided by the **rhētor** and with a variety of attitudes toward education voiced by the Romans themselves.

2. Words to be deduced: **omittere** (18), **abōmin-**

andus (28), **terribilis** (31), **procācitās** (35), and **territus** (37).

3. Structures

    a. Condensed sentence:
      Prīmum ad Thrāciam (nāvigāvērunt),
      deinde Dēlum (nāvigāvērunt),
      tum ad Crētam nāvigāvērunt. (19—20)

    b. Intruding verb: . . . **novam condere Trōiam.** (22—23)

    c. Linking **quī: Quem ubi.** . . . (25).

4. From the very beginning of the course there has been ample exposure to the use of prepositional place constructions, e.g., **in hortō, ad Forum,** and **ab urbe.** This chapter seeks to consolidate and teach the rules for place constructions which do not use prepositions. Such expressions have been deduced in stories as early as Chapter 7: **Rōmam redīre vult** (15). More difficult examples have been given as vocabulary items, e.g., **domum** (22:13—14), **domō** (Exercise 22f, No. 8), **domī** (25:36), and **Brundisiī** (34:4). (See above, Chapter 34, Student's Book, note 4.) All the examples in this story are readily deducible, e.g., **Carthāginī** (13), which follows the question **Quō in locō?,** and **Dēlum** (20), which is enclosed between prepositional phrases (**ad Thrāciam** and **ad Crētam**). Students may ask when encountering the latter example why **Dēlum** does not have a preposition, too. The text was written to prompt this very question.

    It may be noted that we use the usual locative form **Carthāginī,** although Vergil once uses **Carthāgine** (*Aenid* IV.224).

5. As with place constructions, words and phrases expressing time (especially those in the ablative) have been seen many times from the beginning of the course, e.g., **aestāte** (1:2). Ablative words and phrases of time were discussed in a note on page 64 of the first student's book. Accusative expressions of time were introduced in the second student's book, e.g., **abhinc duās hōrās** (24:13), and they have been used with increasing frequency in more recent chapters, e.g., **decem annōs** (36:4). Students should therefore have no difficulty translating expressions like **multōs annōs** in the present chapter (18—19).

6. Lines 17—21 are especially suitable for dictation, containing a minimum of dialogue and a number of place constructions.

7. Vocabulary: Some place names are given, either because they might be unfamiliar to students or because it is important to note their genitive singulars. Attention should be directed to the map included with this chapter, to locate these places and to trace Aeneas' journey.

8. Exercise 37a: Two of these questions prompt more than one correct answer: No. 3, . . . **quod novam Trōiam condere volēbat** or . . . **quod ā dīs monitus est**; and No. 5, **"Nōnne est Graecia?"** or **"Nīl interest."**

9. *Place Clues:* We have tried to simplify the rules for place constructions. The emphasis is on reading strategies rather than on rules for translating English into Latin, although the latter will be clear from the presentation. We divide our presentation into consideration of place words in the *accusative case* (top half of page 80) and of place words in cases *other than the accusative* (bottom half of page 80 and top of page 81). We believe that this is the crucial distinction for reading purposes. In distinguishing between place *from which* and place *in which* with words that do not use prepositions, we urge that students pay attention not only to the ending of the noun but (perhaps even more importantly) to the verb (is it a verb of "motion" or of "rest"?—see top of page 81). To develop good reading habits, students must be sensitive to both the ending of the noun and the meaning of the verb.

    It may be mentioned that **domus** has both 2nd and 4th declension forms and that the 2nd declension ablative singular ending in **-ō** is more frequently used than the 4th declension ending in **-ū**.

10. Exercise 37b: Students may need to be reminded of the phenomenon of plural place names, e.g., **Bāiae, Gādēs,** and **Philippī** here and **Athēnae** in Exercise 37c, No. 8 and Exercise 37e, line 11. Modern examples include Cedar Rapids (Iowa), White Plains (New York), Los Angeles (California), and Trois-Rivières (Quebec).

11. Exercise 37c, Nos. 7 and 8: The teacher may wish to provide some background on Hannibal, the Carthaginian general, who captured Saguntum, a city in Spain allied with Rome, and thus precipitated the Second Punic War (218—201 B.C.). See *The Oxford Classical Dictionary*, "Hannibal," p. 487. **Lūcius Aemilius Paulus Macedonicus** led the Romans to triumph over Macedonia in northern Greece in 168 B.C. at the battle of Pydna. See *The Oxford Classical Dictionary*, "Paullus (2) Macedonicus," pp. 791—792. It may be mentioned to students that Rome's defeat of Hannibal and subsequent triumphs in the East laid the foundations of the Empire as it existed at the time of our story. For Horace's journey in No. 10, see the second student's book, pp. 22—24.

12. *Time Clues:* Time expressions which use prepositions present no difficulty for students, e.g., **post multōs diēs,** *after many days.* The absence of a preposition (or adverb) in time expressions requires the student to distinguish between expressions of time *when* or *within which* clued by the ablative and those of time *how long* (duration) clued by the accusative. As with place constructions, the meaning of the *verb* can be helpful, although the case is decisive, e.g., **Paucīs diēbus perveniet,** "He will arrive in a few days"; **Paucōs diēs morābitur,** "He will stay for a few days."

    Students' attention should be drawn to the distinction between the prepositional and adverbial uses of **ante** and **post**. As prepositions, they govern the accusative, e.g., **post multōs annōs**, "after many years" and **ante prīmam lūcem**, "before dawn." As adverbs, they are associated with the ablative of time *when*, e.g., **multīs post annīs** "many years afterward (later)" (Exercise 37c, No. 3); **tribus post diēbus**, "three days later" and **tribus ante diēbus**, "three days before."

13. *Vergil and the Epic:* For brief retellings of the stories of the *Iliad* and the *Odyssey*, see *Mythology*, pp. 255–318, and/or *Myths of the Greeks and Romans*, pp. 27–96. Students should be encouraged to read these summaries and to compare the Greek heroes Achilles and Odysseus with the Roman hero Aeneas. For Aeneas against the background of the Greek epics and Roman History, see *Myths of the Greeks and Romans*, "The Quest for a New Home," pp. 325–348. There are excellent topics here for essays in English.

14. Exercise 37e:
    a. Phrase to be deduced: **sextus decimus** (3)
    b. Partitive genitive with superlative adjective: **poētārum Rōmānōrum** (1)
    c. For the **toga virīlis** (3–4), see page 14 of the first student's book. Coming of age and the assumption of the **toga virīlis** will be treated in Chapter 50 in the fourth student's book.
    d. Word order: **multīs dē rēbus** (7–8), **est sepultum** (14)
    e. **Augustum** (9): This is the first mention of Augustus in the stories. The relationship between Vergil and the first Roman emperor is worth further discussion and investigation. A brief, factual account of the principate of Augustus, including mention of the Augustan poets, may be found in *The Ancient Romans*, pp. 86–96 (on Augustus) and pp. 104–108 (on the Augustan Age). See also *These Were the Romans*, pp. 146–155, and "Augustus" in *The Oxford Classical Dictionary*, pp. 149–151. For more detail on the life of Vergil (sometimes, chiefly British, spelled *Virgil*), see "Virgil" in *The Oxford Classical Dictionary*, pp. 1123–1128.
    f. **quīnquāgintā annōs nātus** (10): "50 years old." This is an expression of duration of time (*how long*), and literally means "born (perfect participle of **nascor**) for the duration of 50 years."
    g. **Athēnīs** (11, 12): In line 11, **Athēnīs** is ablative of place *where* (not to be read as the dative that goes with **occurrit**), and in line 12 it is ablative of place *from which*.
    h. Linking **quī: Quī** . . . . (11).
    i. **Neāpolim** (14): **-im** was the original ending of the accusative singular of **-i** stem nouns, retained on nouns of Greek origin.

15. The inscription on the tomb of Vergil was said to have been composed by the poet himself just before his death. Calabria is the region in the heel of Italy where Brundisium is located; Parthenope is an old name for Naples, deriving, according to Pliny, from the name of a Siren who was buried there.

16. **Versiculī:** "Back to School," page 103: In line 2, **heu!** is to be deduced.
17. *Roman Education IV:*
    a. The importance of rhetoric or the art of public speaking in the education of a Roman can be emphasized for students by reminding them that in the Roman world—a world of limited literacy and no technological means of communication—the most effective medium of communication was the spoken word. For further information on this and other aspects of Roman education, see the references already cited above, Chapter 34, Student's Book, note 14. For a detailed treatment of Roman higher education, see *Education in Ancient Rome*, Chapter VI, "The Rhetoric Schools and Their Critics," pp. 65–75, and Chapter XVIII, "Progress into Rhetoric," pp. 250–276.

       Debate raged over the effectiveness of the rhetorical schools and the educational value of the staple fare of these schools, which consisted primarily of the students' composing and delivering **contrōversiae**, debates of hypothetical legal cases, and **suāsōriae**, speeches of advice or persuasion addressed to individuals in specific historical situations from the past. These speeches tended to become artificial and devoid of any contact with real life. For a scathing attack on the rhetorical schools, see the selection from Petronius in the cultural background readings at the end of this handbook (p. 47). For a modern treatment of ancient Roman education emphasizing these same weaknesses, see *The Silver-Plated Age*, in which it is argued that "the illiberal liberal education then in vogue stultified the intellect and thus contributed to the marked decline of creativity that signaled the end of ancient civilization" ("Preface").

       A strong contrast to the scholastic artificiality of the rhetorical schools of Petronius' day may be seen in the description which Cicero gives of his rhetorical and philosophical education between the ages of 15 and 25 (91–81 B.C.). This is contained in the extract from his treatise titled *Brutus* that is included on pages 47–48 of the cultural background readings at the end of this handbook. Cicero there recounts how he was always present at the lawcourts even in troubled and dangerous times, how he attached himself to great men of the day to learn civil law, philosophy, and dialectic, and how he practiced rhetorical exercises in the presence of the keenest critics available in order to be thoroughly prepared when he began to plead real cases himself.
    b. Along with the brief extracts illustrating a variety of attitudes to education on pages 85–86 of the student's book, students will enjoy the out-

spoken criticism of education in the first century A.D. contained in the extract from Tacitus in the cultural background readings on pages 46–47 of this handbook.

18. *St. Augustine and Pliny on Education:* These passages should be handled in the same way as those at the ends of Chapters 28, 31, and 33 (see above, Chapter 28, Student's Book, notes 12b–d; Chapter 31, Student's Book, note 10; and Chapter 33, Student's Book, note 10).

Pliny had been asked by a friend, Junius Mauricus, to locate a tutor for his brother's children, and in the extract in the student's book he is daydreaming about returning to school; he thoroughly enjoys both the memories of his own childhood (in stark contrast to St. Augustine!) and the reputation he possesses among schoolboys at the time he is writing the letter.

In the extract from St. Augustine, note that the verb **vāpulāre** is active in form but passive in meaning. In the extract from Pliny, **auctōritātis** is a partitive genitive with **quantum**; the word **auctōritās** refers to the stature and commanding presence of Pliny as a man distinguished by his learning and achievements and to the respectful attitude that he imagines the students having toward him. This is just the opposite of what Messalla complains of in the extract from Tacitus in the cultural background readings (p. 46).

Language Activity Book

1. Activity 37a, No. 6: In the phrase **in urbe Rōmā, Rōmā** is in apposition to **urbe**. This is usually translated into English as "in the city of Rome."
2. Activity 37b: Nos. 8 and 11 give contrasting ways of expressing age in Latin. In No. 8, an ablative of time *(when)* is used with an ordinal number, and the expression means "in this 50th year"; in No. 11, an accusative of duration of time *(how long)* is used with **nātus** and a cardinal number, and the literal meaning is "born for the duration of eight years."
3. Activity 37d: Nos. 1 and 2 underscore the fact that although in English *before* is used both as a preposition and as a subordinating conjunction, in Latin **ante** is the preposition (or adverb) and **antequam** is used to introduce a clause.

   Neāpolī (14): An example of the 3rd declension locative ending in **-ī**.
4. The following is a sample translation of the paragraph in Activity 37e:

Postquam alius discipulus fīnem recitandī fēcit, alius sīc locūtus est: "Aenēās Trōiā profectus," inquit, "multōs annōs errābat: ad Thrāciam, deinde Dēlum, deinde ad Crētam, et tandem ad Siciliam. Nusquam morātus est, sed petēbat Hesperiam, quae terra eadem est ac Italia. Tempestās maxima Aenēān ēgit Carthāginem, quae in Āfricā septentriōnālī ā Dīdōne condita erat. Aenēās amōre cap-

tus multōs diēs ibi morābātur et comitēs miserrimōs nōn animadvertit. Mediā nocte tamen ā dīs monitus Aenēās prīmā lūce ad Italiam profectus est.

CHAPTER 38: TO FATHER FROM SEXTUS

Student's Book

1. a. The present participle was introduced in Chapter 7: **Ibi multōs servōs labōrantēs spectant** (7:4). Students have subsequently seen and used many examples. This chapter introduces the grammatical term *present participle* for the first time and tabulates its forms for regular and deponent verbs. The chapter also contains further practice with perfect passive participles and place clues.
   b. A light, humorous letter concludes the section on Roman education. Like Cornelia's letter in Chapter 34, it recalls the initial chapters of the story and the activities of the children at Baiae. Students will quickly locate and appreciate the humor of Sextus' distortions of the way things actually happened as he attempts to appeal to his father's sympathies.
2. Words to be deduced: **accurrere** (9), **īrācundus** "irritable," "in a bad mood" (17), and **difficilis** (20).
3. The phrase **in marī** in line 4 again shows the ablative singular of neuter i-stem nouns. Cf. **terrā marīque** (36:7–8) and the discussion of i-stem nouns in the second teacher's handbook, Chapter 17, Student's Book, note 13.
4. **scaphās spectāre solēbam** (5): See above, Chapter 31, Student's Book, note 5. This example might be translated simply "I used to watch the boats."
5. The words **rāmō arreptō** (11) are not an ablative absolute. If students find the phrase difficult, ask them to try it without the word **arreptō**.
6. Two subjunctives are introduced (**esset** and **ignōrārem** in line 22, the latter with **cum** causal, "since") without any help with the subjunctives in the vocabulary, since experience has shown that the contextual clues are strong enough to give the sense. The forms may be identified as subjunctives, and students may be alerted to the fact that they will see more forms like this in subsequent chapters and that they will be fully explained in the fourth student's book. Resist the temptation to give a long explanation of the subjunctive at this point. See below, note on Language Activity Book.
7. Some students may need help in translating **eī rogantī** (18), although the shortness of the sentence should make it possible for many to deduce the meaning.
8. **cum prīmum** (24): It is important to stress that this

phrase is to be learned as a unit to avoid unsuitable translations such as "when first."

9. **quam prīmum** (27): The adjective **prīmus, -a, -um** and the adverb **prīmum** are actually superlatives formed from the stem of **prae** or **prō** "before"; see page 67 of the student's book for the translation of **quam** with the superlative adverb.

10. Structures:
    a. Condensed sentences:
       Ibi ad lītus īre (solēbam),
       (ibi) in marī natāre (solēbam),
       (ibi) scaphās spectāre solēbam. (4—5)
       Cēterōs tamen puerōs semper facillima (rogat),
       mē semper difficillima rogat. (19—20)
    b. Word order: **sōlus** at end of sentence for emphasis (12)
    c. Interrupted sentence: **Ille enim homō īrācundissimus mē, quamquam . . . cupiō, saepe. . . .** (16—17)

11. Vocabulary: It should be explained that the verb **audeō** is semideponent, i.e., the forms based on the first two principal parts are not deponent, but in the perfect system it is deponent. Care should be taken that students not try to translate **ausus est** (11) as a passive.

12. In Exercise 38a, No. 4, note the idiom **vēra dīcere,** "to tell the truth."

13. *VERBS: Present Participles:* We give the ablative singular ending as **-e**; the ending in **-ī** will be encountered in readings later in the course.

14. In Exercise 38b, the following points may be noted:
    a. For the **tablīnum** in No. 2, see the plan of the Roman house on page 9 of the student's book.
    b. The subjunctive **esset** (No. 3) should be treated as in note 6 above.
    c. Although some of the present participles can be translated literally, **labōrantī** (No. 5) may be more naturally translated with a relative clause, "who was working."
    d. In several examples, the participle stands on its own (i.e., it does not agree with a noun or pronoun). It is most naturally translated by a noun rather than a participle:
       natantium (No. 7): "of the swimmers"
       gaudentium (No. 11): "of rejoicing" (or "of happy people")

15. **Versiculī:** "Poor Sextus," page 103: Note that in line 1 **Ītaliā** is marked with a long initial *i*, as in Vergil. **Heu!** is to be deduced. The first syllable of **peiōra** (3) is long metrically; the *i* between vowels is consonantal (i.e., *j*) and is doubled in pronunciation, thus making the first syllable long by position.

Language Activity Book

In Activity 38b, No. 4, students are asked to produce subjunctive forms, but they should cause no problem because they are either straight from the reading passage (e.g., **esset**) or easily constructed by analogy with the form in the story (e.g., **Cum Sextus ignōrāret. . . .** in Activity 38b, No. 4, is based on . . . **cum ego ignōrārem. . . .** in 38:22).

WORD STUDY X

1. The aims of this Word Study section are:
   a. to explain the use of the stem of the present participle in the formation of Latin words and English derivatives
   b. to present the Latin suffixes **-ia**, **-īnus**, and **-(i)ānus** and their English derivatives
   c. to explain the use of Latin in medical terminology

2. The note on spellings in **-ant** and **-ent** provides an opportunity to discuss the route by which many words have come from Latin into English and to begin to study the relationship of Latin to the Romance languages. In fact, the majority of English words derived from Latin came into English through French, after the Norman conquest of England in 1066. It is therefore not surprising to find French spellings in English words, the ultimate origin of which is Latin.

3. In Exercise 1, No. 2 is commonly spelled *descendant* as a noun; as an adjective, *descendent* is more common. No. 8 is spelled *defendant*. This exercise illustrates the variety of meanings possible when an English word is used as both an adjective and a noun. For example, No. 5, *patient*, when used as an adjective means "tolerant," but when used as a noun means "someone under medical treatment." Both meanings are related to the basic meaning of **patior:** "to suffer, endure."

4. The role of Latin in medicine has a long and well-established history; a knowledge of Latin terminology has for centuries been essential for the highest paid specialist as well as the simplest country doctor. Latin shares this role in medicine with Greek. Greek is evident in the descriptive aspects of medicine: in the terminology of anatomy, (e.g., *cranium, cardiac*), disease (e.g., *carcinoma, hepatitis*), treatment (*orthopedics, surgery*), and many other areas. The influence of Latin is seen not only in these areas of medicine, but also in the more mundane aspects of daily practice, such as prescribing medication or taking a temporary post for a vacationing doctor, *locum tenens*, "holding the place" of another doctor.

   Student projects on medical Latin might include some of the following:
   a. With the aid of a medical or pharmaceutical dictionary, prepare a number of medical prescriptions using Latin abbreviations.
   b. Ask your family doctor to write some sample medical prescriptions for the class to interpret.
   c. Make a diagram of the human body, labeling the muscles, organs, vascular system, or nervous system with their Latin or Greek names.

d. Find the technical names (drawn usually from Latin or Greek) for some common medical symptoms or disorders, and create a matching exercise for the class, e.g.:

_c_	1. angina pectoris	a.	heart failure
_a_	2. cardiac arrest	b.	bump on the head
_b_	3. subdural hematoma	c.	chest pain

e. Teachers with students whose fathers or mothers are doctors might invite one of them to speak to the class on the use of Latin in the medical profession.

5. For further information on medical Latin, see a medical dictionary such as *Blakiston's Gould Medical Dictionary*. An instructional unit on medical Latin is provided in *Latin, the Language of the Health Sciences*. A *Skeleton Chart* with the principal bones of the body labeled with their Latin names is available from the Teaching Materials and Resource Center of the American Classical League.

CHAPTER 39: BORED

Student's Book

1. **a.** There is no new grammatical material in this chapter, although another subjunctive, **audīvisset** (18), and a perfect infinitive, **discessisse** (14), are given. The latter form is listed in the vocabulary.
   b. The story now returns to Cornelia, whose letter to Flavia we last read in Chapter 34. Her boredom with life in Rome without her friend Flavia and without the boys who are off at school is suddenly dispelled by news from Valerius.

2. Meaning to be deduced: **ēripere** (17), given in Exercise 27c, No. 4, as "to snatch from," here means "to rescue."

3. Structures:
   a. Condensed sentence:
   Īrācunda erat quod Bāiās regredī (cupiēbat) atque (quod) Flāviam amīcam suam vidēre cupiēbat. (2–3)
   b. Emphatic position: **trīstis** (5), **sōla** (7)
   c. Inverted verb: **est morātus** (14)
   d. Linking **quī**: **Quī. . . .** (16)

4. Note the appositive (**amīcam suam**) in line 3. Students should be alert to the fact that appositives will sometimes be found isolated by commas and sometimes not.

5. Cornelia does not attend the secondary school with the boys (see lines 6–9); for the question of the extent to which girls attended Roman secondary schools, see above, Chapter 36, Student's Book, note 11.

6. **tālia** (19): A number of neuter plural adjectives used as substantives have been met throughout the course, e.g., **omnia** (8:4), **multa** (26:18), and **eadem** (35:6). In the sentence **"Quantum mē dēlectat tālia audīre!"** (19), the infinitive **audīre** is the subject of **dēlectat**.

7. In Exercise 39b, No. 2, **templum** and **prōgredī** are to be deduced.

8. *VERBS: Some New Forms:* This note is intended to call students' attention to the new subjunctive forms they have met in the last two chapters. Students are encouraged to note that, although the subjunctive forms are different, their personal endings are the same as those on the indicative verbs they have met. As the note suggests, no discussion of subjunctive or indicative is recommended at this time; the subjunctive will be taken up systematically in the fourth book in this course.

Language Activity Book

1. Activity 39a is a manipulation exercise in which the present participle is seen as a substitute for a relative clause. Students may need guidance in this activity to achieve a full understanding of the process involved in transforming the relative clause into a participial phrase. Teachers are encouraged to establish a step-by-step process that students can use to determine the case, number, and gender of the participle.

   It is instructive to contrast the case of the original relative pronoun with the case of the participle in the revised sentence, e.g., in No. 1 they are both nominative, but in No. 2 **quae** is nominative and the participle required will be accusative. This contrast helps to show students that the participle agrees *completely* with the noun or pronoun it modifies, whereas the relative takes *only* its *number* and *gender* from its antecedent, its case being determined by the function it performs in the clause it introduces.

2. Activity 39c will be a difficult exercise for most students. It should be previewed thoroughly with older students and perhaps done as a class activity with younger ones.

   Students should be encouraged to use participles. For example, in translating the first sentence into English, the structure of the sentence can be changed to "Flavia was unable to go with Cornelia (who was) returning to Rome." This is the way it is translated below and illustrates the preference for compact expression in Latin and full utilization of participles.

   Similarly, the sentence "Flavia left her bedroom . . . and went . . . ." can be recast with a participle: "Flavia, having left her bedroom, went . . . ." Polished Latin prefers this kind of subordination of one idea to another rather than using simple compound sentences.

   Latin also prefers to use a participle with its verbal force rather than a noun. Thus, the sentence, "Father responded in this way to Flavia's question," should be interpreted as "Father responded to Flavia asking."

The following is a sample translation of the paragraph in Activity 39c:

Flāvia cum Cornēliā Rōmam regrediente īre nōn poterat. Flāvia, sōla in cubiculō sedēns, dē amīcā suā optimā cōgitābat. "Quandō," sēcum cōgitābat, "Cornēliam rūrsus vidēbō? Quantum eam dēsīderō!" Eō tempore patrem cum mātre in ātriō loquentem audīvit. Flāvia quam celerrimē ē cubiculō ēgressa in ātrium intrāvit. Cum prīmum parentēs cōnspexit, "Pater māterque," inquit, "hīc prope Bāiās diūtius morātī sumus. Licetne nōbīs Rōmam īre?" Pater Flāviae rogantī respondit sīc: "Fortasse, parvula. Epistulam ad Cornēlium mittam. Sī ille nōs invītāverit, illūc ībimus."

CHAPTER 40: A SLAVE TO THE RESCUE

Student's Book

1. a. There are numerous examples of subjunctives in this fairly long reading passage. The context within which each occurs will make it easy for students to handle them and should convince students that this new form does, indeed, cause little trouble. The grammar note illustrates the perfect active infinitive.

   b. Valerius' slave relates to Flavia and Cornelia the adventures of his master on his voyage from Bithynia to Brundisium and his narrow escape from pirates.

2. Words to be deduced: **pīrāta** (10), **arma** (20), **redūcere** (30–31), and **armātus** (32).

3. Structures:
   a. Intruding verb: . . . **in ingentī erat perīculō**. (4)
   b. Noun-genitive-adjective: . . . **scaphās hominum plēnās** . . . . (8)

4. Students may need help with **suōs** (18) = "his own (men)."

5. Four sentences are future more vivid conditions, using the future or future perfect tense in the conditional clause where English uses a present tense (see the second teacher's handbook, Chapter 22, Student's Book, note 9; and Chapter 25, Student's Book, note 10):

   "Sī mē servāveris, . . . pater meus . . . pecūniam dabit." (11–12)

   "Pīrātae, etiam sī sequentur, nōs nōn capient." (13)

   "Sī pīrātīs resistēmus, . . . necābimur." (19)

   ". . . nisi nōs abīre sinētis, . . . poenās . . . dabitis." (25)

   It may be noted that the sense requires that the verbs in the conditional clauses in the following sentences be in the present tense:

   "Sī pecūniam vultis," inquit, "nūllam pecūniam hīc inveniētis." (23–24)

   "Sī vōs nūllam pecūniam habētis, vōs certē necābimus." (26–27)

6. Note the partitive genitive: . . . **pīrātārum aliī** . . . , **aliī**. . . . (29–30) Compare . . . **alter ē custōdibus** . . . , **alter**. . . . (36) A partitive genitive could have been used with **alter** as well as the construction with **ē** and the ablative.

7. **silentiō** (37): Ablative of manner without a preposition (see the second teacher's handbook, Chapter 24, Student's Book, note 9e).

8. **Iam multōs diēs in scaphā erāmus cum . . . inventī sumus** (41–42): This is the first example in the course of an imperfect tense used in the sense "We had been (and still were). . . ."

9. After reading the story and studying the grammar note on the perfect infinitive, the teacher may introduce the terms *imperfect* and *pluperfect subjunctive* and show how these forms are made from the present and the perfect infinitives, respectively (infinitive + personal ending). The teacher may further point out that the imperfect subjunctive is used for an action going on at the same time as that of the main verb and that the pluperfect subjunctive is used for an action that took place before that of the main verb. The examples in the story clearly show this distinction and may be discussed with the students—*after* the story has been read and translated and the grammar note studied.

10. Opportunity can be taken here to comment on the extent of the Roman Empire at this time (cf. "Eavesdropping" in the second student's book) and on its administration by Roman officials. Valerius had been old enough to accompany his father as a staff officer. Sextus was too young to go with his father. Bithynia should be pointed out on the map on page 81 of the student's book, and a route from there to Brundisium could be traced.

   Piracy was a permanent threat and plague in the ancient world. See *The Oxford Classical Dictionary*, "Piracy," pp. 834–835, and *Piracy in the Ancient World*.

   Pompey in 67 B.C.. acting under provisions of the Gabinian Law, rid the seas—at least temporarily—of the pirates in a remarkable three-month campaign. Piracy resumed during the civil wars, and when Augustus came to power he established a permanent fleet to police the Mediterranean. For Pompey's campaign against the pirates, see the extracts from Cicero's *Manilian Law* in the cultural background readings at the end of this handbook. Students will also be interested in the story of Caesar's capture by the pirates in 74 B.C., which is told by Suetonius, *Caesar* IV.1–2.

   When threatened by the pirates, Valerius invokes his Roman citizenship ("Cīvis sum Rōmānus," 25). For the importance of this claim to

Roman citizenship and the security that it was supposed to afford, see Cicero *Against Verres,* II.V.64.167–168.

11. The illustration on page 96 of the student's book gives a good impression of the different types of sea craft in Roman times. See also the set of ECCE ROMANI posters titled *Travel by Sea.*

12. **Versiculī:** "A Slave to the Rescue," page 104
An ablative absolute occurs in the first line: **acceptō vulnere.** Let students come up with their own translations of it; the words and idea will be familiar to them from **vulnus grave accēpisse vidēbātur** in the story in Chapter 40 (lines 17–18). The ablative absolute will be discussed in the fourth student's book.

13. **Versiculī:** "An Invitation to Dinner," page 104
This is the first of the **versiculī** by an ancient author, already familiar from Chapter 24 of the second student's book. We include it here as an appropriate companion to the chapters on Cornelius' dinner party and also to show students that they can now read "real" Latin with only a moderate amount of vocabulary supplied. This should give students a sense of accomplishment as they reach this point in the Latin program. The meter is phalaecean or hendecasyllabic (see **Versiculī** No. 3 in the first student's book). The poem should be enjoyed for its humorous pseudo-invitation and for its indirect compliment to the poet's girlfriend.
In line 2, note **dī = deī,** as in the familiar **Dī immortālēs!** In line 12, note the plurals, **Venerēs Cupīdinēsque**; students should be encouraged to think of reasons why the poet used the plurals here.

Language Activity Book

1. Activity 40a is intended partly as practice in forming the perfect active infinitive and partly as review of verbs (the students must know their principal parts in order to do this exercise!).

2. The reading passage in Activity 40b contains some present subjunctives (10, 19: **dētur** and **sit**), the former of which is translated in the vocabulary and the latter of which should not cause trouble in context.

REVIEW IX

Student's Book

1. The main grammatical features in Chapters 36–40 that require review are as follows:
   a. numbers (cardinals and ordinals)
   b. place clues
   c. time clues

d. present active participles

2. We do not provide review of imperfect and pluperfect active subjunctives or of perfect active infinitives. These grammatical elements are introduced at the end of the third student's book more as a taste of what is coming in the next book than as new material to be thoroughly mastered at this stage.

3. The exercises in Review IX in the student's book provide review of expressions of place and time and of present active participles. To review cardinal and ordinal numbers, we suggest oral exercises such as the following:
   Respondē Latīnē:
   a. Quotus mēnsis annī est Iānuārius? (Februārius? Martius? Aprīlis? Māius? Iūnius? Iūlius? Augustus? September? Octōber? November? December?)
   b. Quot servōs habet Cornēlius? (1, 2, 3, 4, 5, 6, 7, 8, 9, 10, 11, 12, 20, 50, 100, 500, 1000: the numbers may be written in any order in Arabic or Roman numerals on the board as the teacher repeats the question.)

4. A cumulative review of Books 1–3 is included at the beginning of the fourth teacher's handbook and may be used after Book 3 or before beginning Book 4.

Language Activity Book

In No. 4, a perfect participle of a deponent verb should be used. In No. 5, the relative clause in English may best be rendered with a present participle in Latin. In No. 9 either **petere** or the deponent verb **adorīrī** may be used, but in No. 10 the deponent verb cannot be used. In No. 9, students must remember to use the dative case with the compound verb **appropinquāre.**

The following are sample translations of the sentences in RIXa:

1. Proficīscentēs crās ante prīmam lūcem Tusculum ībimus; paucīs post diēbus Rōmam redībimus.
2. Cornēliī in vīllā prope Bāiās tōtam aestātem manēre nōn poterant.
3. Vīsne Rōmā mēcum tribus diēbus proficīscī, Tite?
4. Paulīsper Carthāginī morātus, Aenēās discessit et ad Italiam nāvigāvit.
5. Duo ē servīs raedam parantibus cistās portābant.
6. Puerī aedificium prope viam stāns vīdērunt.
7. Praedōnēs in aedificiō prope viam stante sē cēlāvērunt.
8. Nōmen aedificiī prope viam stantis erat Amphiteātrum Flāvium.
9. Praedōnēs puerōs aedificiō appropinquantēs adortī sunt (*or* petīvērunt).
10. Puerī petītī domum quam celerrimē fūgērunt.

Addenda to Bibliography

BACKGROUND READINGS

The following books provide further useful background for the cultural topics treated in Book 3:

A History of Private Life: I: From Pagan Rome to Byzantium, ed. by Paul Veyne, tr. by Arthur Goldhammer. Harvard University Press, Cambridge, Massachusetts, 1987. ix + 670 pp.

In particular:

"The Roman Home," "Some Theoretical Considerations," "The Domestic Architecture of the Ruling Class," "'Private' and 'Public' Spaces: The Components of the Domus," "How the Domus Worked," and "Conclusion," pp. 315–409.

As the Romans Did: A Sourcebook in Roman Social History, by Jo-Ann Shelton. Oxford University Press, New York, 1988. xix + 492 pp., paperback.

In particular:

"Single Family Homes in the City," pp. 59–62, "Apartments," pp. 63–64, "Fire Insurance," p. 65, "Meals," pp. 81–87, "Dinner Parties," pp. 315–319, "Patronage," pp. 13–17, "The Problems of City Life," pp. 69–72, and "Education," pp. 104–126.

Civilization of the Ancient Mediterranean: Greece and Rome, ed. by Michael Grant and Rachel Kitzinger. 3 vols. Charles Scribner's Sons, New York, 1988.

In particular:

"Foodstuffs, Cooking, and Drugs," Vol. I, pp. 247–261; "Calendars and Time-Telling," Vol. I, pp. 389–395; "Alphabets and Writing," Vol. I, pp. 397–419; "Book Production," Vol. I, pp. 421–436; "Piracy," Vol. II, pp. 837–844; "Roman Education and Rhetoric," Vol. II, pp. 1109–1120; "Roman Town Houses," Vol. III, pp. 1373–1375; "Ostian Apartment Houses" and "Ostian Town Houses," Vol. III, pp. 1378–1383.

Pompeii: Nowadays and 2000 Years Ago, by Alberto Carlo Carpiceci. American Classical League, Miami University, Oxford, OH. 111 pp., richly illustrated in color. A magnificent survey of the city and buildings of ancient Pompeii, with particular attention to houses.

"Pompeii," a 27" x 39" color reconstruction of the city of Pompeii in A.D. 79, with photographic reproductions of all the buildings. American Classical League, Miami University, Oxford, OH.

TEACHER'S AIDS

The American Classical League offers packets of mimeographs, many of which are useful to teachers of ECCE ROMANI. The following packets of mimeographs contain items of use in teaching Book 3:

M1. Mimeos on Caesar, Cicero, and Vergil.
M2. Mimeos on First Year Latin.
M3. Mimeos on Latin Club, Projects, and Games.
M4. Mimeos on Plays, Productions, and Readings in English and Latin.
M6. Mimeos on Rome and the Romans.
M8. Mimeos on Value of the Classics.
M9. Mimeos on Word Study and Derivation.

Each mimeo is identified by a number, and some mimeos are included in more than one packet. The mimeos are not available individually, but only as packets. The following mimeos, identified by packet code and mimeo number, are particularly useful in teaching Book 3:

"A Visit to a Roman House: A Short Story in Easy Latin," by P. J. Downing (M2 and 4 #114): a brief visit to a Roman house; may be read along with Book 3, pp. 9–11, "Town House and Tenement."

"How to Prepare and Serve a Roman Banquet" (M3 #94): background information on Roman banquets; detailed directions for serving a Roman banquet; menus; and an account of a Roman banquet given by a classical club. Very useful along with Book 3, Chapter 31, "At Dinner," especially if a banquet is held in conjunction with study of this chapter.

"Ten Ancient Recipes from Cato's *De agri cultura*," by Lillian Lawler (M3 and 6 #264): supplements Book 3, pp. 36–39, "Recipes and Menus."

"Latin Derivatives and Phrases in the Legal Vocabulary" (M8 and 9 #574): numerous examples of legal words and phrases in English derived or taken over directly from Latin, with their meanings; useful supplement to the discussion of Latin in the law in Book 3, pp. 56–57.

"Roman Conquests," by Robert Fink (M1, 3, 6, and 8 #740): the second part of this article offers an interesting discussion of the Roman origins of our calendar and may be used with Book 3, Chapter 34, especially, "Dates," and with Exercise 36b. The first half deals with the ancient origins of our alphabet, and this material may easily be brought in as a sidelight to the discussion of the origin of our calendar.

"Schools of Greece and Rome," by C. A. Beard and W. G. Carr (M6 #524): an interesting discussion of schooling in Sparta and Athens and of how the Athenian educational system was transplanted to Rome and modified to meet the needs of the Romans. The emphasis here on Greek schools will allow students to make comparisons with the Roman educational system described in Book 3, Chapters 35 to 37.

"Classical Languages in Medical Education," by L. Lind (M8 #685): the importance of study of Latin, Greek, and etymology for those planning to enter the medical profession. "A Selected List of Latin and Greek Prefixes, Suffixes, Roots, and Abbreviations Used in Medical Terminology" (M8 and 9 #590): a useful list of prefixes and suffixes and their meaning and examples of words in which they are used; a short and interesting list of Latin and Greek derivatives in medical terminology; Latin abbreviations used in medicine, nursing, and pharmacy with full forms spelled out and English meanings; and a short list of Latin and Greek terms used for weights and measures. To accompany Book 3, pp. 92–93, "Latin in Medicine."

The following book will be of use to teachers who wish to enrich the Latin course with material on English grammar:

English Grammar for Students of Latin, by Norma Goldman and Ladislas Szymanski. The Olivia and Hill Press, Inc., P.O. Box 7396, Ann Arbor, MI 48107. 1983. 6 + 202 pp.

   The topics in the following sections of this book will be of particular use in teaching Book 3 of ECCE ROMANI:

   What is a Participle?
   What is Meant by Active and Passive
      Voice?
   What is the Subjunctive Mood?
   What is Meant by Comparison of
      Adjectives?
   What is an Adverb?
   What is a Relative Pronoun?

The Romans Speak for Themselves

For use of these supplementary readers along with the ECCE ROMANI Latin program, see the first teacher's handbook.

   The following lessons in *The Romans Speak for Themselves: Book II* are keyed to the chapters or sections of ECCE ROMANI Book 3 that are given in parentheses:

   Chapter 1. Buildings for Different Ranks of Society
      Vitruvius, *On Architecture* VI.5.1–2
      (after Chapter 27)
   Chapter 2. The *Vigiles*
      Justinian, *Digest* I.15
      (after Chapter 28)
   Chapter 3. The *Commissatio*
      Seneca, *Moral Letters* LXXXIII.24–27
      (after Chapter 32)
   Chapter 4. Violence in the Streets of Rome
      Juvenal, *Satire* III.279–301
      (after Chapter 33)
   Chapter 5. Early Education in Rome
      Quintilian, *The Training of an Orator*
      I.3.8–13
      (after Chapter 37)

Vocabularies

The Vocabulary at the end of the student's book includes all Latin words used in the stories, grammatical notes, and exercises in the student's book. It does not include words which appear only in the culture, word study, and review sections, nor does it include words which appear only in the **versiculī**. The numbers at the left refer to the chapter in which each new word first appears. Words without numbers at the left were introduced in the first or second student's book (except for a few words that appear only in the review sections of the third student's book as words to be deduced; these are included in the end vocabulary in case students need to look them up).

In the Vocabulary at the end of the student's book, the genitive singular of 3rd declension nouns and the principal parts of verbs are abbreviated as they appear in the *Oxford Latin Dictionary*. This system of abbreviation allows students to sound out the full sets of forms with ease and accuracy.

The vocabularies at the end of this teacher's handbook, which may be duplicated and made available to students, are for use in conjunction with Review sections VII, VIII, and IX that follow Chapters 31, 35, and 40 respectively, and the English to Latin translation exercises in the language activity book.

The **Latin Vocabularies** (pages 53–55) are arranged alphabetically by part of speech, with a separate listing of miscellaneous phrases and words that, at this state, need not be grouped into parts of speech. Asterisks indicate words to be mastered.

The **English-Latin Vocabulary** (pages 56–58) is provided to assist students in doing the English to Latin translations in the language activity book.

Cultural Background Readings

THE GREAT FIRE OF ROME: A.D. 64

Tacitus

The following are selections from Tacitus' description of the great fire and its aftermath. The translation is that of John Jackson published in the Loeb Library edition of Tacitus and printed here with the permission of Harvard University Press (all rights reserved). Tacitus (born c. A.D. 56, died c. A.D. 115) was one of Rome's greatest historians; his *Annals* are a history of the Principate from the death of Augustus in A.D. 14 to the end of the year in which Nero committed suicide, A.D. 68.

Reading the following passages to students will inevitably lead to discussion of who was responsible for the great fire. Other questions will also lead to interesting discussions of the topography of Rome, the helplessness of the Roman people, the character of the Emperor, and the historian's own views of the events he is describing. The following specific questions may prove useful:

1. Why was the fire not able to be controlled sooner?
2. What was its effect on the people?
3. Why didn't people try to put the fire out?
4. What impression does Tacitus give of Nero?
5. How does Tacitus use innuendo in alluding to the causes or the person(s) responsible for the first and the second fires?

ANNALS, BOOK XV, CHAPTERS 38–43

There followed a disaster, whether due to chance or to the malice of the sovereign is uncertain—for each version has its sponsors—but graver and more terrible than any other which has befallen this city by the ravages of fire. It took its beginning in the part of the Circus touching the Palatine and Caelian Hills; where, among the shops packed with inflammable goods, the conflagration broke out, gathered strength in the same moment, and, impelled by the wind, swept the full length of the Circus; for there were neither mansions screened by boundary walls, or temples surrounded by stone enclosures, nor obstacles of any description, to bar its progress. The flames, which in full career overran the level districts first, then shot up to the heights, and sank again to harry the lower parts, kept ahead of all remedial measures, the mischief traveling fast, and the town being an easy prey owing to the narrow, twisting lanes and formless streets typical of old Rome. In addition, shrieking and terrified women; fugitives stricken or immature in years; men consulting their own safety or the safety of others, as they dragged the infirm along or paused to wait for them, combined by their dilatoriness or their haste to impede everything. Often, while they glanced back to the rear, they were attacked on the flanks or in front; or, if they had made their escape into a neighboring quarter, that also was involved in the flames, and even districts which they had believed remote from danger were found to be in the same plight. At last, irresolute what to avoid or what to seek, they crowded into the roads or threw themselves down in the fields: some who had lost the whole of their means—their daily bread included—chose to die, though the way of escape was open, and were followed by others, through love for the relatives whom they had proved unable to rescue. None ventured to combat the fire, as there were reiterated threats from a large number of persons who forbade extinction, and others openly throwing firebrands and shouting that "they had their authority"—possibly in order to have a freeer hand in looting, possibly from orders received.

Nero, who at the time was staying in Antium, did not return to the capital until the fire was nearing the house by which he had connected the Palatine with the Gardens of Maecenas. It proved impossible, however, to stop it from engulfing both the Palatine and the house and all their surroundings. Still, as a relief to the homeless and fugitive populace, he opened the Campus Martius, the buildings of Agrippa, even his own Gardens, and threw up a number of extemporized shelters to accommodate the helpless multitude. The necessities of life were brought up from Ostia and the neighboring municipalities, and the price of grain was lowered to three sesterces. Yet his measures, popular as their character might be, failed of their effect; for the report had spread that, at the very moment when Rome was aflame, he had mounted his private stage, and, typifying the ills of the present by the calamities of the past, had sung of the destruction of Troy.

Only on the sixth day was the conflagration brought to an end at the foot of the Esquiline, by demolishing the buildings over a vast area and opposing to the unabated fury of the flames a clear tract of ground and an open horizon. But fear had not yet been laid aside, nor had hope yet returned to the people, when the fire resumed its ravages; in the less congested parts of the city, however; so that, while the toll of human life was not so great, the destruction of temples and porticos dedicated to pleasure was on a wider scale. The second fire produced the greater scandal of the two, as it had broken out on the Aemilian property of Tigellinus and appearances suggested that Nero was seeking the glory of founding a new capital and endowing it with his own name. Rome, in fact, is divided into fourteen regions, of which four remained intact, while three were laid level with the ground: in the other seven nothing survived but a few dilapidated and half-burned relics of houses. . . .

In the capital, however, the districts spared by the palace were rebuilt, not, as after the Gallic fire (390 B.C.), indiscriminately and piecemeal, but in measured lines of streets, with broad thoroughfares, buildings of restricted height, and open spaces, while colonnades were added as a protection to the front of the tenement-blocks. These colonnades, Nero offered at this own expense, and also to hand over the building-sites, clear of rubbish, to the owners. He made a further offer of rewards, proportioned to the rank and resources of the various claimants, and fixed a term within which houses or blocks of tenements must be completed, if the bounty was to be secured. As the receptacle of the refuse, he settled upon the Ostian Marshes and gave orders that

vessels which had carried grain up the Tiber must run downstream laden with debris. The buildings themselves, to an extent definitely specified, were to be solid, untimbered structures of Gabine or Alban stone, that particular stone being proof against fire. Again, there was to be a guard to ensure that the water-supply—intercepted by private lawlessness—should be available for public purposes in greater quantities and at more points; appliances for checking fire were to be kept by everyone in the open; there were to be no joint partitions between buildings, but each was to be surrounded by its own walls. These reforms, welcomed for their utility, were also beneficial to the appearance of the new capital. Still, there were those who felt that the old form had been more salubrious, as the narrow streets and high-built houses were not so easily penetrated by the rays of the sun; while now the broad expanses, with no protecting shadows, glowed under a more oppressive heat.

TRIMALCHIO'S DINNER PARTY

Petronius

At the end of Chapter 31 we have given a brief extract in Latin from Petronius' description of Trimalchio's dinner party. The story of the pig, from which that extract was taken, is given below in its proper sequence along with other excerpts from Petronius' work. Almost everything about Petronius seems open to debate, but he is often identified with the **arbiter elegantiae** at Nero's court, named Petronius. What we possess is fragments of a novel, the *Satyricon*, describing the adventures of a fictional pair, Encolpius, who serves as narrator, and his friend, Giton. In the longest of the surviving episodes, the **cēna Trimalchiōnis**, this disreputable pair and a professor of rhetoric named Agamemnon attend Trimalchio's banquet. The excerpts which follow neatly parallel the order in which things take place at the dinner given by Cornelius. The exaggeration and extravagance of everything at Trimalchio's party will amuse students, and Petronius' observant and satirical eye reveals much about the ways and manners of the Romans. The following excerpts are printed here with permission from the translation by William Arrowsmith in the New American Library (all rights reserved).

THE *SATYRICON:* EXCERPTS

Drunk with admiration, we brought up the rear and Agamemnon joined us when we reached Trimalchio's door. Beside the door we saw a sign:

ANY SLAVE LEAVING THE PREMISES
WITHOUT AUTHORIZATION FROM THE MASTER
WILL RECEIVE ONE HUNDRED LASHES!

At the entrance sat the porter, dressed in that same leek-green that seemed to be the livery of the house. A cherry-colored sash was bound around his waist and he was busily shelling peas into a pan of solid silver. In the doorway hung a cage, all gold, and in it a magpie was croaking out his welcome to the guests.

I was gaping at all this in open-mouthed wonder when I suddenly jumped with terror, stumbled, and nearly broke my leg. For there on the left as you entered, in fresco, stood a huge dog straining at his leash. In large letters under the painting was scrawled:

BEWARE OF THE DOG!

The others burst out laughing at my fright. . . . In the corner at the end of the portico was a huge wardrobe with a small built-in shrine. In the shrine were silver statuettes of the household gods, a Venus in marble, and a gold casket containing, I was told, the clippings from Trimalchio's first beard. . . .

We approached the dining room next where we found the steward at the door making up his accounts.

At last we took our places. Immediately slaves from Alexandria came in and poured ice water over our hands. These were followed by other slaves who knelt at our feet and with extraordinary skill pedicured our toenails. Not for an instant, moreover, during the whole of this odious job, did one of them stop singing. This made me wonder whether the whole menage was given to bursts of song, so I put it to the test by calling for a drink. It was served immediately by a boy who trilled away as shrilly as the rest of them. In fact anything you asked for was served with a snatch of song, so that you would have thought you were eating in a concert-hall rather than a private dining room.

Now that the guests were all in their places, the hors d'oeuvres were served, and very sumptuous they were. Trimalchio alone was still absent, and the place of honor—reserved for the host in the modern fashion—stood empty. But I was speaking of the hors d'oeuvres. On a large tray stood a donkey made of rare Corinthian bronze; on the donkey's back were two panniers, one holding green olives, the other, black. Flanking the donkey were two side dishes, both engraved with Trimalchio's name and the weight of the silver, while in dishes shaped to resemble little bridges there were dormice, all dipped in honey and rolled in poppyseed. Nearby, on a silver grill, piping hot, lay small sausages, while beneath the grill black damsons and red pomegranates had been sliced up and arranged so as to give the effect of flames playing over charcoal.

I turned back to my neighbor to pick up what gossip I could and soon had him blabbing away. . . .

At this point Trimalchio heaved himself up from his couch and waddled off to the toilet. Once rid of our table tyrant, the talk began to flow more freely. Damas called for larger glasses and led off himself. "What's one day? Bah, nothing at all. You turn round and it's dark. Nothing for it, I say, but to jump right from bed to table. Brrr. Nasty spell of cold weather we've been having. A bath hardly warmed me up. But a hot drink's the best overcoat of all; that's what I always say. Whoosh, I must have guzzled gallons. I'm tight and no mistake. Wine's gone right to my head. . . ."

But when the tables had been wiped—to the inevitable music, of course—servants led in three hogs rigged out with muzzles and bells. According to the head-waiter, the first hog was two years old, the second three, but the third was all of six. I supposed that we would now get tumblers and rope dancers and that the pigs would be put through the kind of clever tricks they perform for the crowds in the street. But Trimalchio dispelled such ideas by asking, "Which of these hogs would you like cooked for your dinner? Now your ordinary country cook can whip you up a chicken or make a Bacchante mincemeat or easy dishes of that sort. But my cooks frequently broil calves whole." With this he had the cook called in at once, and without waiting for us to choose our pig, ordered the oldest one slaughtered. Then he roared at the cook, "What's the number of your corps, fellow?"

"The fortieth, sir," the cook replied.

"Were you born on the estate or bought?"

"Neither, sir. Pansa left me to you in his will."

"Well," barked Trimalchio, "see that you do a good job or I'll have you demoted to the messenger corps."

The cook, freshly reminded of his master's power, meekly led the hog off toward the kitchen, while Trimalchio gave us all an indulgent smile. "If you don't like the wine," he said, "we'll have it changed for you. I'll know by the amount you drink what you think of it. Luckily too I don't have to pay a thing for it. It comes with a lot of other good things from a new estate of mine near town. I haven't seen it yet, but I'm told that it adjoins my lands at Terracina and Tarentum. Right now what I'd really like to do is buy up Sicily. Then I could go to Africa without ever stepping off my own property. . . ."

He was still chattering away when the servants came in with an immense hog on a tray almost the size of the table. We were, of course, astounded at the speed and swore it would have taken longer to roast an ordinary chicken, all the more since the pig looked even bigger than the one served to us earlier. Meanwhile Trimalchio had been scrutinizing the pig very closely and suddenly roared, "What! What's this? By god, this hog hasn't even been gutted! Get that cook in here on the double!"

Looking very miserable, the poor cook came shuffling up to the table and admitted that he had forgotten to gut the pig.

"You *forgot*?" bellowed Trimalchio. "*You forgot to gut a pig?*" "And I suppose you think that's the same thing as merely forgetting to add salt and pepper. Strip that man!"

The cook was promptly stripped and stood there stark naked between two bodyguards, utterly forlorn. The guests to a man, however, interceded for the chef. "Accidents will happen," they said, "please don't whip him. If he ever does it again we won't say a word for him." My own reaction was anger, savage and unrelenting. I could barely restrain myself and leaning over, I whispered to Agamemnon, "Did you ever hear of anything worse? Who could forget to gut a pig? By god, you wouldn't catch me letting him off, not if it was just a fish he'd forgotten to clean."

Not so Trimalchio, however. He sat there, a great grin widening across his face and said: "Well, since your memory's so bad, you can gut the pig here in front of us all." The cook was handed back his clothes, drew out his knife with a shaking hand and slashed at the pig's belly with crisscross cuts. The slits widened out under the pressure from inside, and suddenly out poured, not the pig's bowels and guts, but link upon link of tumbling sausages and blood puddings.

The slaves saluted the success of the hoax with a rousing, "LONG LIVE GAIUS!" The vindicated chef was presented with a silver crown and honored by the offer of a drink served on a platter of fabulous Corinthian bronze.

Meanwhile someone was hammering at the door and before long a carouser dressed in a splendid white robe and accompanied by a throng of slaves made his entrance. His face was dignified and stern, so stern in fact that I took him for a praetor, slammed my bare feet onto the cold floor and made ready to run for it. But Agamemnon laughed at my fright and said, "Relax, you idiot, it's only Habinnas. He's an official of the imperial cult and a mason by trade. They say he makes first-rate tombstones."

Somewhat reassured, I sat down again but continued to observe Habinnas' entrance with mounting amazement. He was already half-drunk and was propping himself up by holding onto his wife's shoulders with both hands. He was literally draped in garlands of flowers and a stream of perfumed oil was running down his forehead and into his eyes. When he reached the place reserved for the praetor, he sat down and called for wine and warm water. Trimalchio was delighted to see his friend in such spirits and called for bigger glasses asking him how he had eaten.

"Only one thing was missing," Habinnas smiled, "and that was you. My heart was really here the whole time. But, by god, Scissa did it up brown. She put on one fine spread for that poor slave's funeral, I'll say that for her. What's more, she set him free after his death. And what with the 5 percent tax, I'll bet that gesture cost her a pretty penny. The slave himself was valued at about two thousand. Still, it was very nice, though it cut across my grain to have to pour out half my drinks as an offering to the poor boy's bones."

"But what did they give you to eat?" Trimalchio pressed him.

"If I can remember, I'll tell you," said Habinnas. "But my memory's so bad these days, I sometimes can't even remember my own name. Let's see, first off we had some roast pork garnished with loops of sausages and flanked with more sausages and some giblets done to a turn. And there were pickled beets and some wholewheat bread made without bleach. I prefer it to white, you know. It's better for you and less constipating too. Then came a course of cold tart with a mixture of some wonderful Spanish wine and hot honey. I took a fat helping of the tart and scooped up the honey generously. Then there were chickpeas and lupins, no end of filberts, and an apple apiece. I took two apples and I've got one wrapped up in my napkin here. If I forgot to bring a little present to my pet slave, I'd be in hot water. And oh yes, my wife reminds me: the main course was a roast of bearmeat. Scintilla was silly enough to try some and almost chucked up her supper. But it reminds me of roast boar, so I put down about a pound of it. Besides, I'd like to know, if bears eat men, why shouldn't men eat bears? To wind up, we had some soft cheese, steeped in fresh wine, a snail apiece, some tripe hash, liver in pastry boats and eggs topped with more pastry and turnips and mustard and beans boiled in the pod and—but enough's enough. Oh yes, and they passed around a dish of olives pickled in caraway, and some of the guests had the nerve to walk off with three fistfuls. But we sent back the ham untasted."

Once the confusion had died down, Trimalchio ordered the dessert brought on. The servant immediately removed not merely the dirty dishes but the tables themselves and replaced them with fresh ones. The floor was sprinkled with saffron sawdust and powdered mica, something I had never seen used for this purpose before. "Behold your dessert, gentlemen, these fresh tables," said Trimalchio. "I've made a clean sweep of everything and that's all you get. That's what you deserve; that's your dessert. Haw, haw. But if there's still anything in the kitchen worth eating, boys, bring it on."

The servants brought on another course, consisting of pastry thrushes with raisin and nut stuffing, followed by quinces with thorns stuck in them to resemble sea urchins. We could have put up with these dishes, if the last and most sickening course of all had not killed our appetites completely. When it was first brought in, we took it for a fat goose surrounded by little fish and little birds of all kinds. But Trimalchio declared, "My friends, everything you see on that platter has been made from one and the same substance." I, of course, not a man to be deceived by appearances, had to turn and whisper to Agamemnon, "I'd be very surprised if everything there hadn't been made out of plain mud or clay. At the Carnival in Rome, I've seen whole meals made from stuff like that."

In no time at all the water had cleared the wine fumes from our heads, and we were taken into a second dining room where Fortunata had laid out some of her prize possessions. There was a number of curious lamps, but I particularly remember several figurines of fishermen in bronze and some tables of solid silver covered with gilded goblets into which fresh wine was being strained before our eyes. "My friends," said Trimalchio, apropos of nothing, "my pet slave is having his first shave today. He's a good boy and a model of thrift. So let's celebrate. We'll drink until dawn!"

THE COMMISSATIO AND SOCIAL DRINKING

Plato

Plato (c. 429–347 B.C.), the Greek philosopher and follower of Socrates, in his dialogue titled the *Symposium* or *Drinking Party* (176), has the guests express themselves as follows on how they should drink after their dinner. The translation is that of B. Jowett, reprinted here with permission of Oxford University Press (all rights reserved).

Socrates took his place on the couch, and supped with the rest; and then the libations were offered, and after a hymn had been sung to the god, and there had been the usual ceremonies, they were about to commence drinking, when Pausanias said, And now my friends, how can we drink with least injury to ourselves? I can assure you that I feel severely the effect of yesterday's potations, and must have time to recover; and I suspect that most of you are in the same predicament, for you were at the party yesterday. Consider then: How can drinking be made easiest?

I entirely agree, said Aristophanes, that we should, by all means, avoid hard drinking, for I was myself one of those who were yesterday drowned in drink.

I think that you are right, said Eryximachus, the son of Acumenus; but I should still like to hear one other person speak: Is Agathon able to drink hard?

I am not equal to it, said Agathon.

Then, said Eryximachus, the weak heads like myself, Aristodemus, Phaedrus, and others who never can drink, are fortunate in finding that the stronger ones are not in a drinking mood. (I do not include Socrates, who is able either to drink or to abstain, and will not mind, whichever we do.) Well, as none of the company seem disposed to drink much, I may be forgiven for saying, as a physician, that drinking deep is a bad practice, which I never follow, if I can help, and certainly do not recommend to another, least of all to any one who still feels the effects of yesterday's carouse.

I always do what you advise, and especially what you prescribe as a physician, rejoined Phaedrus the Myrrhinusian, and the rest of the company, if they are wise, will do the same.

It was agreed that drinking was not to be the order of the day, but that they were all to drink only so much as they pleased.

Xenophon

Another Athenian, Xenophon (c. 428–354 B.C.), a man of a more practical and active disposition than his countryman Plato, also wrote about Socrates and also wrote a *Symposium* about an imaginary dinner party with Socrates as one of the guests. Socrates gives the following recommendations (II.24–26) about drinking. The translation is that of O. J. Todd in the Loeb Classical Library edition of Xenophon and printed here with permission of Harvard University Press (all rights reserved).

Here Socrates again interposed. "Well, gentlemen," said he, "so far as drinking is concerned, you have my hearty approval; for wine does of a truth 'moisten the soul' and lull our griefs to sleep just as the mandragora does with men, at the same time awakening kindly feelings as oil quickens a flame. However, I suspect that men's bodies fare the same as those of plants that grow in the ground. When God gives the plants water in floods to drink, they cannot stand up straight or let the breezes blow through them; but when they drink only as much as they enjoy, they grow up very straight and tall and come to full and abundant fruitage. So it is with us. If we pour ourselves immense draughts, it will be no long time before both our bodies and our minds reel, and we shall not be able even to draw a breath, much less speak sensibly; but if the servants frequently 'besprinkle' us—if I too may use a Gorgian expression—with small cups, we shall thus not be driven on by the wine to a state of intoxication, but instead shall be brought by its gentle persuasion to a more sportive mood."

Cicero

Cicero (106–43 B.C.), Roman orator and statesman and admirer and transmitter of Greek culture of the Roman world, in his *De senectute* (XIV) has the Elder Cato (234–149 B.C.) speak in his old age of his fondness for the **commissātiō**, of the prescribed customs for drinking and the opportunity for talk. The following translation is that of William Armistead Falconer published in the Loeb Classical Library edition of Cicero and printed here with permission of Harvard University Press (all rights reserved).

For my own part, because of my love of conversation, I enjoy even "afternoon banquets," not with my contemporaries only, very few of whom now remain, but also with you and those of your age; and I am profoundly grateful to old age, which has increased my eagerness for conversation and taken away that for food and drink. But if there are any who find delight in such things (that I may by no means seem to have declared war on every kind of pleasure, when, perhaps a certain amount of it is justified by nature), then I may say that I am not aware that old age is altogether wanting in appreciation of even these very pleasures. Indeed I find delight in the custom established by our forefathers of appointing presidents at such gatherings; and in the talk, which, after that ancestral custom, begins at the head of the table when the wine comes in; and I enjoy cups, like those in Xenophon's *Symposium*, that are small in size, filled with dew-like drops, cooled in the summer, and, again, in water,

warmed by the heat of the sun or fire. Even when among the Sabines I keep up the practice of frequenting such gatherings, and every day I join my neighbors in a social meal which we protract as late as we can into the night with talk on varying themes.

Horace

The poet Horace (65–8 B.C.) writes as follows in praise of wine drunk in moderation (*Odes* I.18.1–9). The translation is that of C. E. Bennett published in the Loeb Classical Library edition of Horace and printed here with permission of Harvard University Press (all rights reserved). The Centaurs' contest with the Lapiths referred to by Horace took place when Peirithous, king of the tribe of Lapiths in Thessaly, invited the uncouth Centaurs to his wedding feast. The latter were not used to drinking, and their leader, Eurytus, inflamed first with wine and then with lust for Peirithous' bride, provoked a drunken brawl that caused widespread bloodshed among the guests at the banquet (see Ovid, *Metamorphoses* XII.210–535).

O Varus, plant no tree in preference to the sacred vine about the mellow soil of Tibur and by the Walls of Catilus! For to the abstemious has the god ordained that everything be hard, nor are cankering cares dispelled except by Bacchus' gift. Who, after this wine, harps on the hardships of campaigns or poverty? Who does not rather glorify thee, O Father Bacchus, and thee, O comely Venus? And yet, that no one pass the bounds of moderation in enjoying Liber's gifts, we have a lesson in the Centaurs' contest with the Lapithae, fought out to the bitter end over the festal board.

Seneca

Seneca, the Roman moralist (c. 4 B.C.–A.D. 65), who himself practiced abstinence from wine and believed that "it is easier for the will to cut off certain things utterly than to use them with restraint" (*Letters* CVIII.16), scorned the victor in drinking at the **commissātiō** as follows (*Letters* LXXXIII.24–27), using as his example Mark Antony (c. 83–31 B.C.), the triumvir, who upon breaking with Octavian and consorting with the Egyptian queen Cleopatra was finally defeated by Octavian as an enemy of the Roman state at the battle of Actium in 31 B.C. Seneca sees a connection between Antony's drinking and his character and actions in public life. The translation is that of Richard M. Gummere published in the Loeb Classical Library edition of Seneca and printed here with permission of Harvard University Press (all rights reserved).

What glory is there in carrying much liquor? When you have won the prize, and other banqueters, sprawling asleep or vomiting, have declined your challenge to still other toasts; when you are the last survivor of the revels; when you have vanquished every one by your magnificent show of prowess and there is no one who has proved himself of so great capacity as you—you are vanquished by the cask. Mark Antony was a great man, a man of distinguished ability; but what ruined him and drove him into foreign habits and un-Roman vices, if it was not drunkeness and—no less potent than wine—love of Cleopatra? This it was that made him an enemy of the state; this it was that rendered him no match for his enemies; this it was that made him cruel, when as he sat at table the heads of the leaders of the state were brought in; when amid the most elaborate feasts and royal luxury he would identify the faces and hands of men whom he had proscribed; when, though heavy with wine, he yet thirsted for blood. It was intolerable that he was getting drunk when he did such things; how much more intolerable that he did these things while actually drunk! Cruelty usually follows wine-bibbing; for a man's soundness of mind is corrupted and made savage. Just as a lingering illness makes men querulous and irritable and drives them wild at the least crossing of their desires, so continued bouts of drunkenness bestialize the soul. For when people are often beside themselves, the habit of madness lasts on, and the vices which liquor generated retain their power even when the liquor is gone.

Therefore you should state why the wise man ought not to get drunk. Explain by facts, and not by mere words, the hideousness of the thing, and its haunting evils. Do that which is easiest of all—namely, demonstrate that what men call pleasures are punishments as soon as they have exceeded due bounds.

ROMAN EDUCATION

In Chapters 34–37, we have tried to give an overview of Roman education and to present in the Latin stories scenes typical of the **lūdus grammaticus** in the first century A.D. The following passages provide additional perspectives on Roman education.

Quintilian

Marcus Fabius Quintilianus was born in Spain c. A.D. 30–35 and went to Rome at an early age where he studied under the orator Domitius Afer. He became a prominent rhetorician, teacher, and tutor. The work upon which his fame rests, the *Institutio oratoria*, treats the education of the ideal orator from babyhood to maturity. We give below excerpts from Book I, which deals with the earliest stages of education in the home, the learning of letters, and the study of literature (**grammaticē**). These are the sections most relevant to our own story, which finds Marcus and Sextus attending a **lūdus grammaticus**. The translation is adapted from that of H. E. Butler published in the Loeb Classical Library edition of Quintilian and printed here with permission of Harvard University Press (all rights reserved). We have taken bits and pieces from throughout Book I and assembled them in such a way as to allow the reader to follow Quintilian's main topics and concerns in his treatment of education from babyhood through completion of the **lūdus grammaticus**. There is much here of enduring interest and much that may still provoke lively debate among students, teachers, and parents. It should be explained that education in the Roman world had to do largely with the development of verbal skills—listening, reading, writing, and speaking—and that its aim was to produce men able to function well in public life where those skills were essential to individual success and the maintenance of civilized life in the Roman world. Therefore, when Quantilian talks of training the ideal orator, he is talking about the education generally necessary for successful participation in public life and not training in a narrow specialty.

INSTITUTIO ORATORIA, BOOK I (excerpts)

Above all see that the child's nurse speaks correctly. It is the nurse that the child first hears, and her words that he will first attempt to imitate. Do not allow the boy to become accustomed even in infancy to a style of speech which he will subsequently have to unlearn.

As regards parents, I should like to see them as highly educated as possible, and I do not restrict this remark to fathers alone. We are told that the eloquence of the Gracchi owed much to their mother Cornelia, whose letters even today testify to the cultivation of her style. And even those who have not had the fortune to receive a good education should not for that reason devote less care to their son's education but should on the contrary show all the greater diligence.

As regards the **paedagōgus**, I would urge that he should have had a thorough education.

I prefer that a boy should begin with Greek, because Latin, being in general use, will be picked up by him whether we want him to or not. The fact that Latin learning is derived from Greek is a further reason for his being first instructed in the latter. The study of Latin ought to follow at no great distance and in a short time proceed side by side with Greek.

Some hold that boys should not be taught to read until they are seven years old, that being the earliest age at which they can derive profit from instruction and endure the strain of learning. Those however who hold that a child's mind should not be allowed to lie fallow for a moment are wiser.

I am not however so blind to differences of age as to think that the very young should be forced on prematurely or given real work to do. Above all things we must take care that the child, who is not yet old enough to love his studies, does not come to hate them and dread the bitterness which he has once tasted, even when the years of infancy are left behind. His studies must be made an amusement: he must be questioned and praised and taught to rejoice when he has done well; sometimes too, when he refuses instruction, it should be given to some other to excite his envy, at times also he must be engaged in competition and should be allowed to believe himself successful more often than not, while he should be encouraged to do his best by such rewards as may appeal to his tender years.

I am not satisfied with the course (which I note is usually adopted) of teaching small children the names and order of the letters before their shapes. Such a practice makes them slow to recognize the letters, since they do not pay attention to their actual shape, preferring to be guided by what they have already learned by rote. I quite approve on the other hand of a practice which has been devised to stimulate children to learn by giving them ivory letters to play with (as I do of anything else that may be discovered to delight the very young), the sight, handling, and naming of which is a pleasure.

As regards syllables, no short cut is possible: they must all be learned, and there is no good in putting off learning the most difficult; this is the general practice, but the sole result is bad spelling. The syllables once learned, let the child begin to construct words with them and sentences with the words.

But the time has come for the boy to grow up little by little, to leave the nursery and tackle his studies in good earnest. This therefore is the place to discuss the question as to whether it is better to have him educated privately at home or hand him over to some large school and those whom I may call public instructors. Let me explain my own preference for public instruction. It is above all things necessary that our future orator, who will have to live in the utmost publicity and in the broad daylight of public life, should become accustomed from his childhood to move in society without fear and habituated to a life far removed from that of the pale student, the solitary and recluse. His mind requires constant stimulus and excitement. At school he will hear many merits praised and many faults corrected every day: he will derive equal profit from hearing the indolence of a comrade rebuked or his industry commended. Such praise will incite him to emulation; he will think it a disgrace to be outdone by his contemporaries and a distinction to surpass his seniors. It is a good thing that a boy should have companions whom he will desire first to imitate and then to surpass: thus he will be led to aspire to higher achievement.

The skillful teacher will make it his first care, as soon as a boy is entrusted to him, to ascertain his ability and character. The surest indication in a child is his power of memory. The indication of next importance is the power of imitation: for this is a sign that the child is teachable. My ideal pupil will absorb instruction with ease and will even ask some questions; but he will follow rather than anticipate his teacher. Precocious intellects rarely produce sound fruit. Give me the boy who is spurred on by praise, delighted by success, and ready to weep over failure. Such a boy must be encouraged by appeals to his ambition; rebuke will bite him to the quick; honor will be a spur, and there is no fear of his proving indolent.

I disapprove of flogging, although it is the regular custom, because in the first place it is a disgraceful form of punishment and fit only for slaves, and is in any case an insult, as you will realize if you imagine its infliction at a later age. Secondly if a boy is so insensible to instruction that reproof is useless, he will, like the worst type of slave, merely become hardened to blows. Finally, there will be absolutely no need of such punishment if the teacher is a thorough disciplinarian.

I will now proceed to describe the subjects in which the boy must be trained, if he is to become an orator, and to indicate the age at which each should be commenced.

As soon as the boy has learned to read and write without difficulty, it is the turn for the teacher of literature (**grammaticus**). My words apply equally to Greek and Latin teachers, though I prefer that a start should be made with a Greek: in either case the method is the same. This profession may be most briefly considered under two heads, the art of speaking correctly and the interpretation of the poets. But there is more beneath the surface than meets the eye. For the art of writing is combined with that of speaking, and correct reading precedes interpretation, while in each of these cases critical ability has its work to perform.

Nor is it sufficient to have read the poets only; every kind of writer must be carefully studied, not merely for the subject matter, but for the vocabulary; for words often acquire authority from their use by a particular author. Nor can such

training be regarded as complete if it stops short of music, for the teacher of literature has to speak of meter and rhythm; nor again, if he be ignorant of astronomy, can he understand the poets; for they frequently give their indications of time by reference to the rising and setting of the stars. Ignorance of philosophy is an equal drawback, since there are numerous passages in almost every poem based on the most intricate questions of natural philosophy. For these reasons, those who criticize the art of teaching literature as trivial and lacking in substance put themselves out of court. Unless the foundations of oratory are well and truly laid by the teaching of literature, the superstructure will collapse. The study of literature is a necessity for boys and a delight of old age, the sweet companion of our privacy and the sole branch of study which has more solid substance than display.

The elementary stages of the teaching of literature (**grammaticē**) must not therefore be despised as trivial. It is of course an easy task to point out the difference between vowels and consonants, and to subdivide the latter into semivowels and mutes. The next subject to which attention must be given is that of syllables. Following this the teacher will note the number and nature of the parts of speech, although there is some dispute as to their number. Boys should begin by learning to decline nouns and conjugate verbs: otherwise they will never be able to understand the next subject of study. This admonition would be superfluous but for the fact that most teachers, misled by a desire to show rapid progress, begin with what should really come at the end: their passion for displaying their pupils' talents in connection with the more imposing aspects of their work serves but to delay progress, and their shortcut to knowledge merely lengthens the journey.

Having stated the rules which we must follow in speaking, I will now proceed to lay down the rules which must be observed when we write. Such rules are called *orthography* by the Greeks; let us style it the science of writing correctly. For my own part, I think that, within the limits prescribed by usage, words should be spelled as they are pronounced. For the use of letters is to preserve the sound of words and to deliver them to readers as a sacred trust: consequently they ought to represent the pronunciation which we are to use.

Reading remains for consideration. In this connection there is much that can only be taught in actual practice, as for instance when the boy should take breath, at what point he should introduce a pause into a line, where the sense ends or begins, when the voice should be raised or lowered, what modulation should be given to each phrase, and when he should increase or slacken speed, or speak with greater or less energy. In this portion of my work, I will give but one golden rule: to do all these things, he must understand what he reads.

Above all, unformed minds are liable to be all the more deeply impressed by what they learn in their days of childish ignorance, and they must learn not merely what is eloquent; it is even more important that they should study what is morally excellent. It is therefore an admirable practice which now prevails, to begin by reading Homer and Vergil, although the intelligence needs to be further developed for the full appreciation of their merits: but there is plenty of time for that since the boy will read them more than once. In the meantime, let his mind be lifted by the sublimity of heroic verse, inspired by the greatness of its theme, and imbued with the loftiest sentiments.

In lecturing, the teacher of literature (the **grammaticus**) must give attention to minor points as well: he will ask his class after analyzing a verse to give him the parts of speech and the peculiar features of the feet which it contains. He will point out what words are barbarous, what improperly used, and what are contrary to the laws of the language. In the elementary stages of such instruction it will not be unprofitable to show the different meanings which may be given to each word.

In addition to this, the teacher will explain the various stories that occur: this must be done with care but should not be encumbered with superfluous detail. For it is sufficient to set forth the version which is generally received or at any rate rests upon good authority. But to ferret out everything that has ever been said on the subject even by the most worthless of writers is a sign of tiresome pedantry or empty ostentation and results in delaying and swamping the mind when it would be better employed on other themes.

I will now proceed briefly to discuss the remaining arts in which I think boys ought to be instructed before being handed over to the teacher of rhetoric: for it is by such studies that the course of education described by the Greeks as general education (*enkyklios paideia*) will be brought to its full completion.

Let us discuss the advantages which our future orator may reasonably expect to derive from the study of music. Music has two modes of expression—in the voice and in the body (i.e., in dance). For both voice and body require to be controlled by appropriate rules. I think I ought to be emphatic in stating that the music which I desire to see taught is not our modern music, which has been emasculated by the lascivious melodies of our effeminate stage and has to no small extent destroyed such manly vigor as we still possessed. No, I refer to the music of old which was employed to sing the praises of brave men and was sung by the brave themselves. I will have none of your psalteries and viols, that are unfit even for the use of a modest girl. Give me the knowledge of the principles of music, which have power to excite or assuage the emotions of mankind.

As regards geometry, it is granted that portions of this science are of value for the instruction of children: for admittedly it exercises their minds, sharpens their wits, and generates quickness of perception. But it is considered that the value of geometry resides in the process of learning, and not as with other sciences in the knowledge thus acquired. Such is the general opinion. But it is not without good reason that some of the greatest men have devoted special attention to this science. It will suffice for our purpose that there are a number of problems which it is difficult to solve in any other way, which are as a rule solved by these linear demonstrations, such as the method of division, section to infinity, and the ratio of increase in velocity. From this we may conclude that, if an orator has to speak on every kind of subject he can under no circumstances dispense with a knowledge of geometry.

The comic actor will also claim a certain amount of our attention, but only in so far as our future orator must be a master of the art of delivery. The teacher borrowed from the comic stage will in the first place correct all faults of pronunciation and see that the utterance is distinct and that each letter has its proper sound.

I will not blame even those who give a certain amount of time to the teacher of gymnastics. I am not speaking of those who spend part of their life in rubbing themselves with oil and part in wine-bibbing and kill the mind by over-attention to the body: indeed, I would have such as these kept as far as possible from the boy whom we are training. But we give the same name to those who form gesture and motion so that the

arms may be extended in the proper manner, the management of the hands free from all trace of rusticity and inelegance, the attitude becoming, the movements of the feet appropriate, and the motions of the head and eyes in keeping with the poise of the body. No one will deny that such details form a part of the art of delivery, nor divorce delivery from oratory.

I trust that there is not even one among my readers who would think of calculating the monetary value of such studies. He who has enough of the divine spark to conceive the ideal eloquence, he who, as the great tragic poet Pacuvius says, regards "oratory" as "the queen of the world" and seeks not the transitory gains of advocacy but those stable and lasting rewards which his own soul and knowledge and contemplation can give, *he* will easily persuade himself to spend his time not, like so many, in the theater or in the Campus Martius, in dicing or in idle talk, to say nothing of the hours that are wasted in sleep or long-drawn banqueting, but in listening rather to the geometrician and the teacher of music. For by this he will win a richer harvest of delight than can ever be gathered from the pleasures of the ignorant, since among the many gifts of providence to man not the least is this that the highest pleasure is the child of virtue.

Such are the studies in which a boy must be instructed, while he is yet too young to proceed to greater things.

Tacitus

Quintilian's recommendations are idealized and admittedly often at variance with the educational practice of his day. Tacitus (c. A.D. 56–c. 115), in his *Dialogue on Oratory* has Messalla, one of the participants in the dialogue, comment as follows on the shortcomings of contemporary education (the fictional date of the dialogue is A.D. 74). The following translation is adapted from that of W. Peterson and M. Winterbottom published in the Loeb Classical Library edition of Tacitus and printed here with permission of Harvard University Press (all rights reserved).

CHAPTER 29
"Nowadays . . . our children are handed over at their birth to some silly little Greek serving-maid, with a male slave, who may be anyone, to help her—quite frequently the most worthless member of the whole establishment, incompetent for any serious service. It is from the foolish tittle-tattle of such persons that the children receive their earliest impressions, while their minds are still green and unformed; and there is not a soul in the whole house who cares a jot what he says or does in the presence of his baby master. Yes, and the parents themselves make no effort to train their little ones in goodness and self-control; they grow up in an atmosphere of laxity and pertness, in which they come gradually to lose all sense of shame and all respect both for themselves and for other people. Again, there are the peculiar and characteristic vices of this metropolis of ours, taken on, as it seems to me, almost in the mother's womb—the passion for play actors and the mania for gladiatorial shows and horse-racing; and when the mind is engrossed in such occupations, what room is left over for higher pursuits? How few are to be found whose home-talk runs to any other subjects than these? What else do we overhear our younger men talking about whenever we enter their lecture-halls? And the teachers are

just as bad. With them, too, such topics supply material for gossip with their classes more frequently than any others; for it is not by the strict administration of discipline, or by giving proof of their ability to teach that they get pupils together, but by pushing themselves into notice at morning calls and by the tricks of toadyism."

Petronius

Debate raged in the Roman world over the effectiveness of the rhetorical schools (see Chapter 37) which young men attended after graduating from the **lūdus grammaticus**. The terms of this debate are clearly seen in the following exchange between Encolpius and Agamemnon in Petronius' *Satyricon* (1–4). Encolpius has been listening to Professor Agamemnon declaiming in the rhetoric school and can stand it no longer. Again, the translation is that of William Arrowsmith:

"No one would mind this claptrap if only it put our students on the road to real eloquence. But what with all these sham heroics and this stilted bombast you stuff their heads with, by the time your students set foot in court, they talk as though they were living in another world. No, I tell you, we don't educate our children at school; we stultify them and then send them out into the world half-baked. And why? Because we keep them utterly ignorant of real life. The common experience is something they never see or hear. All they know is pirates trooping up the beach in chains, tyrants scribbling edicts compelling sons to chop off their fathers' heads or oracles condemning three virgins—but the more the merrier—to be slaughtered to stop some plague. Action or language, it's all the same; great sticky honeyballs of phrases, every sentence looking as though it had been plopped and rolled in poppyseed and sesame. A boy gorged on a diet like this can no more acquire real taste than a cook can stop stinking. What's more, if you'll pardon my bluntness, it was you rhetoricians who more than anyone else strangled true eloquence. By reducing everything to sound, you concocted this bloated puffpaste of pretty drivel whose only real purpose is the pleasure of punning and the thrill of ambiguity. Result? Language lost its sinew, its nerve. Eloquence died. . . ."

Agamemnon, however, refused to let me rant on an instant longer than it had taken him to sweat out his declamation in the classroom. "Young man," he broke in, "I see that you are a speaker of unusual taste and, what is even rarer, an admirer of common sense. So I shan't put you off with the usual hocus-pocus of the profession. But in all justice allow me to observe that we teachers should not be saddled with the blame for this bombast of which you complain. After all, if the patients are lunatics, surely a little professional lunacy is almost mandatory in the doctor who deals with them. And unless we professors spout the sort of twaddle our students admire, we run the risk of being, in Cicero's phrase, "left alone at our lecterns." Let me offer you by way of analogy those professional sponges in the comic plays who scrounge their suppers by flattering the rich. Like us they must devote their entire attention to one end—the satisfaction of their audience; for unless their little springes con their listeners' ears, they stand to lose their quarry. We are, that is, rather in the position of a fisherman: unless he baits the hook with the sort of tidbit the fishes like, he is doomed to spend eternity sitting on his rock without a chance of a bite.

Cicero

In the following extract from the *Brutus* (304–312), Cicero tells of his rhetorical and philosophical education (see above, Chapter 37, Student's Book, note 17a). The translation is that of G. L. Hendrickson in the Loeb Classical Library edition of Cicero and is printed here with permission of Harvard University Press (all rights reserved).

In the first year of the war the only court still active was taken up by cases under a single law, the Varian; all others because of the war were suspended. At its hearings I was present constantly, and though the accused speaking in their own defense where not orators of the first rank—men like Lucius Memmius and Quintus Pompeius, still they were orators; and there was one at least really eloquent, Philippus, witness against the accused, whose vehemence in testimony had all the force and eloquence of a prosecutor.

The first blow to my eagerness to hear fell with the banishment of Cotta. I continued however to listen to those who were left, and though I wrote and read and declaimed daily with unflagging interest, yet I was not satisfied to confine myself only to rhetorical exercises. In the year following Quintus Varius went into exile, a victim of his own law. I meantime, for the study of civil law, attached myself to Quintus Scaevola, the son of Quintus, who though he took no pupils, yet by the legal opinions given to his clients taught those who wished to hear him. The year following this was the consulship of Sulla and Pompeius. Publius Sulpicius was tribune and addressed the people almost daily, so that I came to know his style thoroughly. At this time Philo, then the head of the Academy, along with a group of loyal Athenians, had fled from Athens because of the Mithridatic war and had come to Rome. Filled with enthusiasm for the study of philosophy I gave myself up wholly to his instruction. In doing so I tarried with him the more faithfully, for though the variety and sublimity of his subject delighted and held me, yet it appeared as if the whole institution of courts of justice had vanished forever. In that year Sulpicius had fallen, and in the year following three orators representing three different periods met a cruel death, Quintus Catulus, Marcus Antonius, Gaius Julius. At this time too I devoted myself to study at Rome with Molo of Rhodes, famous as a pleader and teacher. . . .

For a space of about three years the city was free from the threat of arms. . . . During all this time I spent my days and nights in study of every kind. I worked with Diodotus the Stoic, who made his residence at my house, and after a life of long intimacy died there only a short time ago. From him, apart from other subjects, I received thorough training in dialectic, which may be looked upon as a contracted or compressed eloquence. . . . But though I devoted myself to his teaching and to a wide range of subjects at his command, yet I allowed no day to pass without some rhetorical exercises. I prepared and delivered declamations (the term now in vogue), most often with Marcus Piso and Quintus Pompeius, or indeed with anyone, daily. This exercise I practised much in Latin, but more often in Greek, partly because Greek, offering more opportunity for stylistic embellishment, accustomed me to a similar habit in using Latin, but partly too because the foremost teachers, knowing only Greek, could not, unless I used Greek, correct my faults nor convey their instruction. . . .

It was my ambition, not (as most do) to learn my trade in the forum, but so far as possible to enter the forum already trained. At this time too I devoted myself to study with Molo; for it chanced that he came to Rome in the dictatorship of Sulla as a member of a commision to the senate with regard to the reimbursement of Rhodes. Thus my first criminal case, spoken on behalf of Sextus Roscius, won such favorable comment that I was esteemed not incompetent to handle any litigation whatsoever.

PIRACY

Cicero

In 66 B.C. when the Roman campaign against Mithridates, king of Pontus, had stalled under the leadership of Lucullus, the tribune Manilius introduced a bill to transfer command of the Roman forces to Pompey. Cicero in his speech in favor of the bill recounted Pompey's success against the pirates the previous year (67 B.C.). The following extracts from the passage on the war against the pirates are adapted from the translation of H. Grose Hodge published in the Loeb Classical Library and are printed here with permission of Harvard University Press (all rights reserved). As our passage begins, Cicero is citing evidence of Pompey's ability as a commander by describing how extensively the Mediterranean had been infested with pirates prior to his command against them:

PRO LEGE MANILIA 32–35
But why do I remind you of events in distant places? There was a time long ago when it was Rome's peculiar boast that the wars she fought were far from home and that the outposts of her empire were defending the prosperity of her allies, not the homes of her own citizens. Need I mention that the sea during these wars was closed to our allies, when your own armies never made the crossing from Brundisium save in the depth of winter? Need I lament the capture of envoys on their way to Rome from foreign countries, when ransom has been paid for the ambassadors of Rome? Need I mention that the sea was unsafe for merchantmen, when twelve lictors have fallen into the hands of pirates? Need I record the capture of the noble cities of Cnidus and Colophon and Samos and of countless others, when you well know that your own harbors and those, too, through which you draw the very breath of your life, have been in the hands of the pirates? Are you indeed unaware that the famous port of Caieta, when crowded with shipping, was plundered by the pirates under the eyes of the praetor, and that from Misenum the children of the very man who had previously fought there against the pirates were kidnapped by the pirates?

Is it possible that the incredible, the superhuman genius of a single man has in so short a time illumined the darkness which beset his country, that you, who but lately saw with your eyes a hostile fleet before the Port of Tiber, now hear the news that there is not a pirate ship within the Portal of Ocean? The rapidity with which this feat was accomplished you all know, but I cannot omit to mention it in my speech. For who, however eager for the transaction of business or the pursuit of gain, has ever succeeded in visiting so many places in so short a time or in accomplishing such long journeys at the same speed with which, under the leadership of Pompey, that mighty armament swept over the seas? Pompey, though the sea was still unfit for navigation, visited Sicily, explored Africa, sailed to Sardinia, and, by means of strong garrisons and fleets, made secure those three sources of our country's grain supply. After that he returned to Italy, secured the two provinces of Spain together with Transalpine Gaul, dispatched ships to the coast of the Illyrian Sea, to Achaea and the whole of Greece, and so provided the two seas of Italy with mighty fleets and strong garrisons; while he himself, within forty-nine days of starting from Brundisium, added all Cilicia to the Roman Empire. All the pirates, wherever they were, were either captured and put to death or they surrendered to his power and authority and to his alone.

Bibliography and Useful Information for Teachers

I. BOOKS AND ARTICLES REFERRED TO IN THE TEACHER'S HANDBOOK

Note that references have been restricted to books that are currently in print. Many other resources can be found in libraries. Asterisks in the list below mark books regarded as highly recommended for the school library. Double asterisks mark books that should be available as basic resources in the Latin classroom.

Ancient Roman Feasts and Recipes: Adapted for Modern Cooking, by Jon and Julia Solomon. E. A. Seeman, Miami, FL, 1977. illustrated.

Apicius: Cookery and Dining in Imperial Rome, by Joseph Dommers Vehling. Peter Smith, Magnolia, MA *or* Dover, Mineola, NY, 1977, paperback. Background information on Apicius and translation of recipes. Source book for the teacher and interested students.

**Aspects of Roman Life Folder A*. Longman, New York, 1975. Contains 32 yellow source sheets, 4 sheets of photos, 1 sheet of plans, 2 sheets of models, and 8 double-sided work cards on 16 different topics (4 copies of each work card per set of materials). To accompany the booklets titled *Roman Towns, The Roman House*, and *Roman Family Life* in the Longman "Aspects of Roman Life" series. Suitable for late elementary grades and junior high school.

Black's Law Dictionary, by Henry C. Black. West Publishing Co., St. Paul, MN, 1979. 1511 pp. Also abridged edition, 1983. 855 pp. A standard reference for Latin legal expressions and their application in legal practice.

Blakiston's Gould Medical Dictionary. McGraw-Hill Book Co., NY, 1979. illustrated. A standard reference work.

Classical Mythology, by Mark P. O. Morford and Robert J. Lenardon. Longman, White Plains, NY, 1985 (3rd edition). xviii + 544 pp., paperback. A standard, college-level textbook with ancient sources in translation.

Daily Life in Ancient Rome; The People and the City at the Height of the Empire, by Jerome Carcopino, edited by Henry T. Rowell, translated by E. O. Lorimer. Yale University Press, New Haven, CT, 1940. xi + 342 pp., paperback. A detailed study of Roman life; background for the teacher and an excellent resource for students' projects.

Education in Ancient Rome: From the Elder Cato to the Younger Pliny, by Stanley F. Bonner. University of California Press, Berkeley, CA, 1977. xii + 404 pp., illustrated, paperback. A comprehensive, scholarly, carefully documented treatment. Specialized background for the teacher; source material for students' reports.

Food and Drink, by Kenneth McLeish. "Greek & Roman Topics" series. George Allen & Unwin, Boston, 1978. 64 pp., illustrated, paperback. General background; suitable for high school students.

Houses, Villas and Palaces in the Roman World, by A. G. McKay. "Aspects of Greek and Roman Life" series. Cornell University Press, Ithaca, NY, 1975. 288 pp., illustrated. An excellent reference work for high school students and teachers.

How to Prepare and Serve a Roman Banquet. American Classical League, Oxford, OH. Mimeograph; Order number M 94. 4 pp. Background information, practical suggestions, menus.

Latin, the Language of the Health Sciences, by Rudolph Masciantonio. American Classical League, Oxford, OH. Order number B 313. 42 pp., paperback. Latin expressions used in anatomy, pharmacology, and medicine; English derivatives and cognates; the Greco-Roman heritage in the health sciences.

Law and Life of Rome: 90 B.C. to A.D. 212, by J. A. Crook. "Aspects of Greek and Roman Life" series. Cornell University Press, Ithaca, NY, 1984. 352 pp., paperback. A comprehensive study of Roman law and legal practice. Primarily for the teacher.

Legal Latin: Teacher's Guide, by Rudolph Masciantonio. American Classical League, Oxford, OH. Order number B 312. 82 pp., paperback. Latin maxims and phrases used in modern law; English derivatives and cognates; the Greco-Roman heritage in law; passages on law from Greek and Latin literature.

Mythology, by Edith Hamilton. Little, Brown and Company, Boston, 1942. New American Library (Mentor), NY, 1971. The myths retold; suitable for junior and senior high school students.

Mythology and You: Classical Mythology and Its Relevance to Today's World, by Donna Rosenberg and Sorelle Baker. National Textbook Company, Lincolnwood, IL, 1981. 295 pp., paperback. A textbook suitable for high school or college; emphasis on personal response to the myths.

Myths and Their Meanings, by Max J. Herzberg. Allyn and Bacon, Inc., Boston, 1984. ix + 357 pp., illustrated, paperback. A high school level textbook.

Myths of the Greeks and Romans, by Michael Grant. New American Library (Mentor), NY, 1964. paperback, illustrated. Suitable for high school students.

Petronii Arbitri Cena Trimalchionis, ed. by Martin S. Smith. Oxford University Press, New York, 1975. xxxvi + 233 pp. The Latin text with extensive notes.

Pictorial Dictionary of Ancient Rome, by Ernest Nash. Frederick A. Praeger: now distributed by Hacker Art Books, NY, 1961, (2nd ed., revised). Volume I, 544 pp., Volume II, 535 pp., both lavishly illustrated. An authoritative pictorial survey of the monuments and ruins of ancient Rome, arranged alphabetically. Extremely useful.

Piracy in the Ancient World: An Essay in Mediterranean History, by Henry A. Ormerod. State Mutual Book & Periodical Service, NY, 1982. 286 pp. A comprehensive treatment; background for the teacher.

Roman Family Life, by Peter Hodge, "Aspects of Roman Life" series. Longman, New York, 1974. 62 pp., illustrated, paperback. A student's textbook for study of Roman culture; contains discussions of various topics, quotations of ancient sources, illustrations, study questions, and suggestions for projects. Suitable for late elementary and junior high school.

**Roman Life*, by Mary Johnston. Scott, Foresman and Company, Glenview, IL, 1957. 478 pp., illustrated. Very informative; excellent reference work for high school students and teachers. A useful resource book for students' projects.

Roman Towns, by Peter Hodge. "Aspects of Roman Life" series. Longman, New York, 1977. 48 pp., illustrated, paperback. Same comments apply as to *Roman Family Life* above.

Rome and Environs, edited by Alta Macadam. "Blue Guide" series. W. W. Norton, New York, 1979 (2nd ed.). 402 pp., plus maps, illustrated, paperback. A detailed and authoritative guide to the city and its environs with an emphasis on the ancient monuments.

**Rome: Its People, Life and Customs*, by Ugo Enrico Paoli, translated by R.D. Macnaghten. Longman, New York, 1963. xiii + 336 pp., illustrated. Excellent, detailed, well-documented accounts of all major aspects of Roman culture. A basic background book for students and teachers to use in conjunction with ECCE ROMANI. Suitable for high school students and teachers.

Ten Ancient Recipes from Cato's De Agri Cultura, by Lillian Lawler. American Classical League, Oxford, OH. Mimeograph; Order number M 264. 3 pp. Recipes in Latin and English translation.

The Ancient Romans, by Chester G. Starr. Oxford University Press, NY, 1971. illustrated, paperback. A comprehensive treatment.

The Oxford Classical Dictionary, ed. by N. G. L. Hammond and H. H. Scullard. Oxford University Press, New York, 1970 (2nd ed.). xxii + 1176 pp. Detailed, scholarly background material for the teacher.

The Roman Cookery of Apicius: A Treasury of Gourmet Recipes & Herbal Cookery Translated and Adapted for the Modern Kitchen, by John Edwards. Hartley & Marks, Point Roberts, WA, 1984. xxx + 322 pp.

The Roman House, by Peter Hodge. "Aspects of Roman Life" series. Longman, New York, 1975. 62 pp., illustrated, paperback. Same comments apply as to *Roman Family Life* above.

The Roman Origins of Our Calendar, by Van L. Johnson. American Classical League, Oxford, OH, 1969. Order number B 406. 80 pp., paperback. Detailed information on the Roman calendar as "a list of festivals and anniversaries on same of which it was *fas* or right to do legal business in the assembly." Teacher reference.

The Silver-Plated Age, by Tom B. Jones. Coronado Press, Sandoval, NM, 1962. 185 pp., paperback. Interesting, provocative background for the teacher.

These Were the Romans, by G. I. F. Tingay and J. Badcock. Dufour Editions, Inc., Chester Springs, PA, 1979. 193 pp., illustrated, paperback. A readable account of many aspects of Roman culture and civilization for high school students.

II. GENERAL BOOKS ON ANCIENT ROME AND ITS CULTURE AND CIVILIZATION

The Civilization of Rome, by Donald R. Dudley. "A Mentor Book." The New American Library, New York, 1962. 256 pp., illustrated, paperback. An account for teachers and mature high school students.

The Romans, by R. H. Barrow. Penguin Books, New York, 1975. 223 pp. A fairly broad, general account of the character of the Romans and their achievements.

The Romans: An Introduction to Their History and Civilization, by Karl Christ. University of California Press, Berkeley, CA, 1984. 275 pp. A detailed, authoritative historical and cultural survey of the Romans.

The Romans and Their World, by Peter D. Arnott. St. Martin's Press, New York, 1970. 318 pp., illustrated, paperback. Interesting background reading for the teacher and mature high school students.

III. BACKGROUND BOOKS FOR WORD STUDY

English Words from Latin and Greek Elements, by Donald M. Ayers. University of Arizona Press, Tucson, AZ,

1980. xiii + 271 pp., paperback. A useful "Introduction" on the Indo-European family of languages and the background of English vocabulary is followed by chapters introducing prefixes, suffixes, and bases and discussing various linguistic phenomena that have shaped the English language. Highly recommended as background for the teacher.

Latin and Greek in Current Use, by Eli E. Burriss and Lionel Casson. Prentice-Hall, Englewood Cliffs, NJ, 1949. xi + 292 pp. An alternative to the book listed above.

*Latin-English Derivative Dictionary, by Rudolf F. Schaeffer. American Classical League, Miami University, Oxford, OH, 1960. 48 pp., paperback. A useful dictionary listing the English derivatives from Latin words.

*Latin Words in Current English, by Graydon W. Regenos. American Classical League, Miami University, Oxford, OH. 54 pp., paperback. Over 7,000 words that have come into English from Latin with few or no changes.

Word Ancestry: Interesting Stories of the Origins of English Words, by Willis A. Ellis. American Classical League, Miami University, Oxford, OH. 62 pp., paperback. Stories of English words, most of them derived from Greek or Latin.

IV. POSTERS AND CLASSROOM ACCESSORIES

"Travel by Sea." Posters, color. Longman, White Plains, NY, 1975. The two posters illustrate Roman trade on the high seas and the many facets of Roman navigational science.

"Roman Calendar." American Classical League, Oxford, OH. Order number A1. A wall calendar for the current school year using the Roman system of dating with prominent Roman dates noted.

The following charts, available from the American Classical League (address above), may be used in conjunction with word study sections in the third student's book of ECCE ROMANI:

**Order number P9. "Derivative Tree Chart." 25" × 19".

**Order number P6. "Legal Terms." Several legal terms in Latin with English translations. 25" × 19".

**Order number P3. "Skeleton Chart." Principal bones of the body labeled with their Latin names. 25" × 19".

V. LATIN LANGUAGE BOOKS

Allen and Greenough's New Latin Grammar for Schools and Colleges, edited by J. B. Greenough, G. L. Kittredge, A. A. Howard, and Benjamin L. D'Ooge. Caratzas Brothers, New Rochelle, NY, 1975. 490 pp., paperback.

Cassell's New Compact Latin Dictionary. Dell Distributing, New York, 1981. 384 pp., paperback.

Cassell's Latin Dictionary, Latin-English, English-Latin, edited by D. P. Simpson. Macmillan Co., New York, 1977.

Latin: A Historical and Linguistic Handbook, by Mason Hammond. Harvard University Press, Cambridge, MA, 1976. ix + 292 pp., paperback. A useful historical and linguistic introduction to Latin written with high school Latin teachers in mind.

Latin Word Lists: Years One Through Four with English Meanings and Instructions in Latin Word Formation, by John K. Colby. Independent School Press, Wellesley Hills, MA, 1978. 47 pp., paperback. Standard listing of words to be mastered in the first four levels of Latin.

New College Latin and English Dictionary, by John C. Traupman. Amsco School Publications, New York, 1966, and Bantam Books, New York, 1970.

**Orbis Pictus Latinus: Illustrated Latin Dictionary*, by Hermann Koller. Longman, New York, 1983. 431 pp., illustrated, paperback. An intriguing dictionary with simple Latin definitions of interesting, culture-laden Latin words.

Oxford Latin Dictionary, edited by P. G. W. Glare. Oxford University Press, New York, 1983. xxiv + 2,126 pp. The definitive Latin dictionary for schools and colleges.

VI. AUDIO-VISUAL RESOURCES

Many audio-visual resources are available, and teachers should take full advantage of them as supplements to the textbook and as additional ways to make the ancient world come alive for students. The quality of films, filmstrips, cassettes, and slides that are available commercially for purchase or rental varies greatly, as does the suitability of these materials for particular levels of instruction and the needs and tastes of particular teachers and groups of students. For full listings of materials available, teachers should consult *The Classical World*, the publication of the Classical Association of the Atlantic States. Periodically, *The Classical World* publishes a "Survey of Audiovisual Materials in the Classics," containing listings and brief descriptions of materials available with prices and addresses of the companies from which the materials may be ordered. Teachers should consult this listing and choose materials that appear to be appropriate to their needs, and they should then request examination copies. The wise teacher will not purchase audio-visual materials sight-unseen but will review a number of possibilities and choose what is most appropriate.

Teachers may also make their own collections of slides to illustrate the various reading passages and cultural topics, drawing on their own photographs taken during travel abroad, or photographs taken in museums in the United States or Canada, or photographs taken from the numerous picture books of ancient Rome and its civilization now available.

VII. ANCIENT SOURCES

Ancient authors have been quoted in some of the cultural readings in the student's book and in most of the quotations in the teacher's handbook from the translations in the Loeb Classical Library series, usually with some adaptations. These translations are published with permission of Harvard University Press (all rights reserved). The following list of authors and works in the Loeb Classical Library series is provided for reference (each volume contains the Latin text and facing translation, plus introduction and notes). The list is alphabetical by name of the author.

Cicero: Pro Lege Manilia, tr. H. Grose Hodge
Petronius, tr. Michael Heseltine
Pliny, tr. Betty Radice
Quintilian, tr. H. E. Butler
Suetonius, tr. J. C. Rolfe
Tacitus: Agricola, tr. M. Hutton and R. M. Ogilvie
Tacitus: The Annals, tr. John Jackson

Principal Parts of Verbs

Following is a list of verbs of which the principal parts are given in the designated chapters (for the purposes of this list, see page 52 of the second teacher's handbook).

29	accipiō	31	dēpōnō	36	obsideō
31	accumbō	38	dēsiliō	28	opprimō
29	addō	32	discēdo	29	pascō
33	adimō	38	discō	36	patior
40	adorior	31	edō	27	pectō
30	afferō	27	effugiō	33	percutiō
37	animadvertō	35	ēgredior	34	persuādeō
38	arcessō	28	ēiciō	32	poscō
38	audeō	27	ēripiō	35	proficīscor
27	aufugiō	40	ēvādō	28	quaerō
36	augeō	36	expellō	38	rapiō
29	bibō	37	expergiscor	27	recumbō
27	capiō	35	experior	36	regō
35	collābor	37	extendō	35	regredior
28	commoveō	32	fīō	38	repellō
32	compleō	32	hauriō	29	reprehendō
30	cōnficiō	36	incendō	40	resistō
35	cōnor	35	ingredior	27	rumpō
35	cōnsequor	36	īnstituō	31	scindō
37	conticēscō	31	irrumpō	37	sepeliō
40	convalēscō	35	loquor	35	sequor
40	coorior	33	lūdō	32	sinō
30	coquō	29	minuō	30	stō
33	corripiō	32	misceō	27	teneō
33	crēdō	37	morior	27	vēndō
38	cupiō	35	moror	35	vereor
36	dēleō	37	nascor	32	vincō

LATIN VOCABULARIES CHAPTERS 27–31

=============== NOUNS ===============

adstantēs	*incendium	*pānis
asparagus	*incola	perna
cachinnus	*īnfāns	pirum
carō	Īnferī	popīna
*convīva	*īnsula	*porcus
*coquus	*iocus	pretium
crīnēs	lanius	pullus
*culīna	lepus	*rēgnum
dēnārius	*lībertus	rixa
*fenestra	*locus	ruīna
ferculum	*mālum	*sella
*fīnis	*memoria	*solea
*flamma	mendīcus	*spectāculum
frustum	*mēnsa	*speculum
*fūmus	neglegentia	trīclīnium
glīs	olīva	īiva
gustātiō	*ōrnāmenta	versus
holus	ōvum	*vestis

=============== VERBS ===============

*accipere	*dēlectāre	*minuere
*accumbere	*dēpōnere	obscūrāre
addere	efferre	*opprimere
addūcere	effugere	pascere
afferre	ēicere	pectere
aufugere	ēmittere	*quaerere
*bibere	ēripere	*recumbere
*capere	esse (to eat)	*reprehendere
captāre	*excūsāre	retinēre
commovēre	exstinguere	*rumpere
comparāre	grunnīre	*scindere
concursāre	*inīre	tremere
*cōnficere	*invītāre	vēndere
*coquere	irrumpere	*vocāre
*dēbēre		

=============== PREPOSITIONS ===============

*circum

=============== ADJECTIVES ===============

celeber	īrātissimus	*parvus
*celerrimus	miserābilis	*pinguis
*cēterī	neglegēns	procāx
*complūrēs	niger	*pulcher
ēlegantissimus	*nōnus	*pulcherrimus
fidēlissimus	nōtus	*quīntus
īnfirmus	ōrnātissimus	vexātus

=============== MISCELLANEOUS ===============

ā servīs ferēbantur	*neglegenter
ac	omnia aguntur
*aut . . . aut	*paene
*autem	*quā dē causā
cōmiter	*Quantī . . . ?
cuius	*quidem
dē porcō datum est	recitāns
Estō!	*rēctē
Euge!	rēs urbānae
*grātīs	*secundae mēnsae
*immō	sine dubiō
in quibus	solent esse incendia
in tertiō tabulātō	*summā celeritāte
*ita	*tam
*magnopere	*umquam
mēcum	*ūnā
*multum	

LATIN VOCABULARIES CHAPTERS 32-35

NOUNS

*adulēscēns   iēntāculum   rosa
*collis   lanterna   *sanguis
*convīvium   *lūdus   Subūra
*cūra   *magister   *tergum
*deus   *modus   *Vergilius
   fūstis   *paedagōgus   *vulnus
*grammaticus

ADJECTIVES

affectus   īrātus   sēcurus
aspersus   *laetus   *sextus
*dīligēns   lentus   situs
*ēbrius   neglegēns   *suāvis
   ērūdītus   *pessimus   *summus
*ferōx   prōnus   *trīstis
   foedus   *prūdēns   *ūtilis
*fortis   *prūdentior   *vehemēns
*gravis   *pulcher   *vetus
*ignāvus   Quirīnālis   *vīgintī

VERBS

adimere   *dēsiderāre   *morārī
castīgāre   *discēdere   percutere
collābī   *ēgredī   *persuādēre
*colloquī   *experīrī   *placēre
complēre   *fierī   *poscere
*cōnārī   haurīre   praeferre
concurrere   indūcere   *proficīscī
condere   *ingredī   regredī
*cōnsequī   invocāre   *sequī
corōnāre   ligāre   *sinere
corripere   *loquī   *verērī
*creāre   *lūdere   *vincere
*crēdere   *miscēre   *vulnerāre
*dēfendere

PREPOSITIONS

*apud   *inter

MISCELLANEOUS

a.d. iii Kal. Dec.   *optimē
   Brundisiī   *paulātim
*celerius   prīdiē Īdūs Octōbrēs
*cotīdiē   *prūdenter
*facile   *quam (as . . . as possible)
*fortissimē   *quam (than)
   Īdibus Novembribus   *quam celerrimē
   in diēs   *-que
   Kalendīs Novembribus   quī hominēs
*libenter   quō . . . eō
*magis   *rūrsus
*maximē   sānē
*memoriā tenēre   sīs
*nē . . . quidem   *vel
*nīl   *vesperī
*nimis   vīnō abstinēns
   Nōnīs Novembribus

POSITIVE, COMPARATIVE, AND SUPERLATIVE ADJECTIVES (REGULAR AND IRREGULAR)

bonus, melior, optimus
facilis, facilior, facillimus
fēlīx, fēlīcior, fēlīcissimus
ignāvus, ignāvior, ignāvissimus
magnus, maior, maximus
malus, peior, pessimus
multī, plūrēs, plūrimī
multus, plūs, plūrimus
parvus, minor, minimus
pulcher, pulchrior, pulcherrimus

POSITIVE, COMPARATIVE, AND SUPERLATIVE ADVERBS (REGULAR AND IRREGULAR)

bene, melius, optimē
celeriter, celerius, celerrimē
dīligenter, dīligentius, dīligentissimē
diū, diūtius, diūtissimē
facile, facilius, facillimē
fēlīciter, fēlīcius, fēlīcissimē
lentē, lentius, lentissimē
magnopere, magis, maximē
male, peius, pessimē
multum, plūs, plūrimum
paulum, minus, minimē
saepe, saepius, saepissimē
sērō, sērius, sērissimē

MONTHS OF THE YEAR

Iānuārius   Māius   September
Februārius   Iūnius   Octōber
Martius   Iūlius   November
Aprīlis   Augustus   December

LATIN VOCABULARIES CHAPTERS 36–40

NOUNS

*Aenēās
Aenēis
*Āfrica
*annus
*arma
*Asia
*bellum
*caelum
Carthāgō
*casa
cithara
comes
Cremōna
Crēta
Dēlos
Dīdō
*discipulus
ferula

fundus
Hesperia
Horātius
*hostis
īrācundia
lāna
*lingua
*lītus
*magister
Mantua
*mare
Mediolānum
*mēnsis
*nāvis
Neāpolis
*oppidum
*pax
*pīrāta

*populus
procācitās
pugiō
*rēgīna
*respōnsum
*rēx
*rogātiō
scapha
Sicilia
*studium
*tempestās
*templum
Thrācia
*Trōia
*Ulixēs
*unda
*ventus
*verbum

ADJECTIVES

abōminandus
*aeger
aliquī
*armātus
*crūdēlis
*difficilis

*dīves
*īrācundus
*paucī
*pauper
septentriōnālis
sextus decimus

*superbus
*terribilis
*territus
Trōiānus
*vērus

VERBS

accurrere
*adorīrī
*aegrōtāre
*animadvertere
*arcessere
*audēre
*augēre
*coepit
conticēscere
convalēscere
coorīrī
*cupere
'dēlēre
dēsilīre
discere

dormitāre
ēvādere
*expellere
expergiscī
extendere
iactāre
*ignōrāre
*īnstituere
interest
migrāre
*monēre
*morī
*nasci
*nāvigāre
obsecrāre

*obsidēre
*occupāre
omittere
*pārēre
*patī
prōgredī
*rapere
redūcere
*regere
repellere
resistere
sepelīre
*studēre
*superāre

PREPOSITIONS

*praeter   *trāns
*propter

MISCELLANEOUS

*antequam
Avē! Avēte!
*clam
*cum (since)
*cum prīmum
fīnem recitandī facere
forās īre
*hieme
īdem ac
*immō vērō
in terram ēgressus
*inde
īnfirmā valētūdine
*multīs post annīs
neque . . . neque . . . quidquam
*nusquam

*poenās dare
*prīmō
Prō dī immortālēs!
*Ouam diū . . . ?
*quam prīmum
*Quantum . . . !
*quoniam
*Quot . . . ?
*Quota hōra est?
*Quotus . . . ?
rēs sacrae
*sīc
*tālia
*vēra dīcere
*vērō

ORDINAL NUMBERS

*prīmus   *octāvus   vīcēsimus
*secundus   *nōnus   quīnquāgēsimus
*tertius   *decimus   centēsimus
*quārtus   ūndecimus   quīngentēsimus
*sextus   duodecimus   mīllēsimus
*septimus

CARDINAL NUMBERS

*ūnus   *septem   vīgintī
*duo   *octō   quīnquāgintā
*trēs   *novem   *centum
*quattuor   *decem   quīngentī
*quīnque   ūndecim   *mīlle
*sex   duodecim

55

Vocabulary for Activities 27e, 29c, 29g, 30d, 31d, RVIIa, 33e, 35d, RVIIIa, 37e, 38b, 39c, and RIXa

able: **posse**
about: **dē** (+ *abl.*)
add: **addere**
affected: **affectus**
afraid: **verērī**
after: **post**
after: **postquam**
again: **iterum**
again: **rūrsus**
all: **omnis**
allow: **licet** + *dat.*
alone: **sōlus**
although: **quamquam**
amphitheater: **amphitheātrum**
amuse: **dēlectāre**
and: **et** or **-que**
another: **alius**
approach: **appropinquāre** (+ *dat.*)
arrive: **advenīre**
as quickly as possible: **quam celerrimē**
as soon as possible: **quam prīmum**
as soon as: **cum prīmum**
as . . . as possible: **quam** + superlative
as: **ac**
as: **ut**
at once: **statim**
at: **ad** (+ *acc.*)
attack: **petere** or **adorīrī**

bad temper: **īrācundia**
be punished: **poenās dare**
beat: **verberāre**
because: **quod**
bedroom: **cubiculum**
before: **ante** (+ *acc.*)
beg: **obsecrāre**
best: **optimus**
better: **melior**
big: **magnus**
bind: **ligāre**
black: **niger**
blood: **sanguis**
boat: **scapha**
boy: **puer**
brave: **fortis**
bring: **afferre**
brother: **frāter**
building: **aedificium**
but: **sed**

butcher: **lanius**
buy: **emere**
by: **ā** or **ab** (+ *abl.*)

can: **posse**
capture: **capere**
careful: **dīligēns**
carelessly: **neglegenter**
carriage: **raeda**
carry: **ferre** or **portāre**
catch sight of: **cōnspicere**
catch up: **cōnsequī**
catch: **captāre**
certainly: **certē**
chest: **cista**
chicken: **pullus**
children: **līberī**
city: **urbs**
client: **cliēns**
club: **fūstis**
collapse: **collābī**
comb: **pectere**
Come on!: **Age!**
come out: **exīre**
companion: **comes**
conceal: **cēlāre**
cook: **coquus**
cookshop: **popīna**
couch: **lectus**
courteous: **cōmis**
courteously: **cōmiter**
cut: **scindere**

dawn: **lūx** or **prīma lūx**
day: **diēs**
delay: **morārī**
delight: **dēlectāre**
depart: **discēdere**
dining room: **triclīnium**
dinner: **cēna**
dirty: **sordidus**
ditch: **fossa**
door: **iānua**
dormouse: **glīs**
doubt: **dubium**
drink: **bibere**
drive: **agere**
during the day: **interdiū**

eight: **octō**
enough: **satis**

enter: **ingredī**
enter: **intrāre**
even: **etiam**
ever: **umquam**
everyone: **omnēs**

fall: **cadere**
farm: **vīlla rūstica**
farmhouse: **vīlla**
fast: **celeriter**
fat: **pinguis**
father: **pater**
fear: **timor**
feed: **pascere**
few: **paucī**
fiercely: **ferōciter**
finally: **tandem**
find: **invenīre**
finish reciting: **fīnem recitandī facere**
flee: **fugere**
follow: **sequī**
for a short time: **paulīsper**
for: **ad** + *acc.*
found: **condere**
freedman: **lībertus**
friend: **amīca**
from there: **inde**
from: **ē** or **ex** (+ *abl.*)

garden: **hortus**
get ready: **parāre**
girl: **puella**
give: **dare**
go in(to): **ingredī** or **intrāre**
go past: **praeterīre**
go: **īre**
god: **deus**
Good!: **Bene!**
great: **magnus**
greatly: **magnopere**
greet: **salūtāre**
guest: **convīva** or **hospes**

hair: **crīnēs**
hall: **ātrium**
hand over: **trādere**
hand: **manus**
happy: **laetus** or **libenter**
hard: **strēnuus**
he: **ille**

hear: **audīre**
help: **adiuvāre**
her (accusative): **eam**
her (possessive): **eius**
her (own): **sua**
her: **eā** (*abl.*)
here (adverb): **hīc**
here (to be here): **adesse**
herself: **ipsa**
him (to him): **eī**
him: **eum**
hire: **condūcere**
his: **eius**
home (at home): **domī**
home (to home): **domum**
hors d'oeuvres: **gustātiō**
How . . . !: **Quam . . . !**
How much . . . !: **Quantum . . . !**
however: **autem** or **tamen**
huge: **ingēns**

if: **sī**
in this way: **sīc**
in: **in** (+ *abl.*)
insolent: **procāx**
intend: **in animō habēre**
into: **in** (+ *acc.*)
invite: **invītāre**

joke: **iocus**

keep back: **retinēre**
kitchen: **culīna**
know (not know): **ignōrāre**
know: **scīre**

land: **terra**
late: **sērō**
laughter: **cachinnus**
lead away: **abdūcere**
lead: **dūcere**
learn: **discere**
learned: **ērūdītus**
leave: **ēgredī ē** (+ *abl.*)
let: **sinere**
letter: **epistula**
light: **lūx**
litter: **lectīca**
little one (*fem.*): **parvula**
load: **onus**
long (for a long time): **diū**
look for: **petere**
loud: **magnus**
love: **amor**

man: **homō**
many: **multī** or **plūrimī**
master of the drinking: **arbiter bibendī**
master: **dominus**

may: **licet** (+ *dat.*)
me (to me): **ad mē**
me (with me): **mēcum**
me: **mē**
meat: **carō**
merchant: **mercātor**
middle (of): **medius**
miss: **dēsiderāre**
mix: **miscēre**
money: **pecūnia**
mother: **māter**
move: **movēre**
must: **necesse est** + *dat.* + *infin.*

name: **nōmen**
near: **prope** (+ *acc.*)
night: **nox**
no one: **nēmō**
northern: **septentriōnālis**
not know: **ignōrāre**
not want: **nōlle**
not . . . even: **nē . . . quidem**
not . . . yet: **nōndum**
not: **nōn**
nothing: **nihil**
notice: **animadvertere**
now: **nunc**
nowhere: **nusquam**

of: **ē** or **ex** (+ *abl.*)
often: **saepe**
old: **vetus**
on account of: **propter** (+ *acc.*)
on: **in** (+ *abl.*)
once: **ōlim**
one: **alius**
one: **ūnus**
only: **modo**
order: **iubēre**
others: **aliī**
out of: **ē** or **ex** (+ *abl.*)
overcome: **affectus**

parent: **parēns**
past (go past): **praeterīre**
perhaps: **fortasse**
pig: **porcus**
place: **pōnere** or **impōnere**
play: **lūdere**
pork: **porcus**
praise: **laudāre**
prepare: **parāre**
price: **pretium**
properly: **rēctē**
pull: **trahere**
punish: **pūnīre**

question: use participle of **rogāre**
quickly: **celeriter**

rabbit: **lepus**
ready: **parātus**
receive: **accipere**
recite: *see* finish reciting
recline: **accumbere** or **recumbere**
remain: **manēre**
remember: **memoriā tenēre**
respond: **respondēre**
rest (the rest): **cēterī**
return: **redīre** or **regredī**
road: **via**
robber: **praedō**
run about: **concursāre**
rush: **sē praecipitāre**

sad: **trīstis**
said: **inquit**
sail: **nāvigāre**
same (the same . . . as): **īdem . . . ac**
school teacher: **grammaticus**
school: **lūdus**
scold: **reprehendere**
scrap: **frustum**
sedan chair: **sella**
see: **vidēre**
sell: **vēndere**
senator: **senātor**
send: **mittere**
sensible: **prūdēns**
serious: **gravis**
set out: **proficīscī**
severe: **vehemēns**
she: **ea**
shop: **taberna**
shore: **lītus**
short (in a short time): **brevī tempore**
short time (for a short time): **paulīsper**
sight: **spectāculum**
signal: **signum**
since: **cum**
sit: **consīdere** or **sedēre**
six: **sex**
slave-woman: **ancilla**
slave: **servus**
small: **parvus**
smile: **rīsus**
some: **aliī**
something: **aliquid**
soon: **mox**
spattered: **aspersus**
speak: **loquī**
stand: **stāre**
stay: **manēre** or **morārī**
stick: **baculum**
storm: **tempestās**
street: **via**
strike: **percutere**

student: **discipulus**
study: **tablīnum**
suddenly: **subitō**
summer: **aestās**

table: **mēnsa**
take: **auferre**
talk: **loquī**
teach: **docēre**
teacher: **grammaticus** or **magister**
temper (bad temper): **īrācundia**
ten: **decem**
test: **experīrī**
than: **quam**
that: **ille**
their: **suus**
them (to them): **eīs**
them: **eōs**
themselves: **sē**
then: **deinde**
there: **ibi**
there: **illūc**
thief: **praedō**
things: use neuter plural of adjective
think: **cōgitāre**
this: **hic**
three: **trēs**
through: **per** (+ *acc.*)

time: **tempus**
to be: **esse**
to herself: **sēcum**
to him: **eī**
to: **ad** (+ *acc.*)
tomorrow: **crās**
too much: **nimis**
tree: **arbor**
try: **cōnārī**
tunic: **tunica**
tutor: **paedagōgus**
two: **duo**

uncle: **patruus**
unhappy: **miser**
unwilling(ly): **invītus**
us: **nōs**
useful: **ūtilis**

verse: **versus**

wagon: **plaustrum**
wait for: **exspectāre**
wait: **morārī**
walk: **ambulāre**
wander: **errāre**
want: **velle**
warn: **monēre**
wash: **lavāre**

watch: **spectāre**
water: **aqua**
way (in this way): **sīc**
well: **bene**
what: **quī**
What . . . ?: **Quid . . . ?**
When . . . ?: **Quandō . . . ?**
when: **cum** or **ubi**
where: **ubi**
which: **quī**
who: **quī**
whole: **tōtus**
wine: **vīnum**
wise: **prūdēns**
wish: **velle**
with: **cum** (+ *abl.*)
without: **sine** (+ *abl.*)
wolf: **lupus**
worried: **sollicitus**
wound: **vulnus**
wound: **vulnerāre**
write: **scrībere**

year: **annus**
Yes!: **Ita vērō!**
yet (not yet): **nōndum**
you (for you): **tibi**
you: **tū**
your: **tuus**

Syntax

I. NOUNS

A. Nominative Case

1. A *predicate noun* or *adjective* after a verb of *calling, making,* or *becoming* in the passive voice is in the nominative case:

> **"'Nōn sine causā tū vocāris Pseudolus.'"** (29:25)
> *"'Not without reason are you called Pseudolus.'"*
> **"Quis creābitur arbiter bibendī?"** (32:5–6)
> *"Who will be chosen master of the drinking?"*
> **Fit in diēs molestior.** (Exercise 32e, line 16)
> *"He becomes more troublesome every day."*

B. Genitive Case

1. The *partitive genitive* is used with superlative adjectives and adverbs (see pages 47 and 53):

> **Titus erat bibendī arbiter pessimus omnium.** (32:29–30)
> *Titus was the worst master of the drinking of all.*
> **Hic puer optimē omnium scrībit.** (Exercise 33g, No. 2)
> *This boy writes best of all.*

C. Dative Case

1. The dative used with the verb **sum** may indicate *possession;* the thing possessed is the subject of the clause and the person who possesses it is in the dative:

> **. . . servus quīdam cui nōmen est Pseudolus.** (29:5–6)
> *. . . a certain slave, to whom the name is Pseudolus,* better English, *whose name is Pseudolus,* or *who has the name Pseudolus.*

D. Ablative Case

1. If the action of a passive verb is carried out by a person, the *ablative of agent* is used, consisting of the preposition **ā** or **ab** with the ablative case:

> **. . . māter et fīlia ā servīs per urbem ferēbantur.** (27:14–15)
> *. . . the mother and her daughter were being carried through the city by slaves.*

Compare the *ablative of means,* consisting of a word or phrase in the ablative without a preposition, that is used when the action is done out by a thing:

> **Vōs omnēs opprimēmimī aut lapidibus aut flammīs.** (28:21)
> *You will all be overwhelmed either with stones or flames.*

You have also seen the ablative of means used with active verbs:

> **Dāvus eum tunicā arripit et baculō verberat.** (12:19–20)
> *Davus grabs hold of him by the tunic and beats him with his stick.*

2. The *ablative of comparison* may be used with comparative adjectives and adverbs (see pages 51 and 53):

> **Martiālis Eucleide est prūdentior.** (Exercise 33d, No. 4)
> *Martial is wiser than Eucleides.*
> **Sextus celerius Marcō currere potest.** (Exercise 33g, No. 4)
> *Sextus can run faster than Marcus.*

3. The ablative case is used to express the *degree of difference* with comparative adjectives, adverbs, and other words implying comparison:

> **"Quam libenter eum rūrsus vidēbō! Sānē tamen multō libentius tē vidēbō ubi tū Rōmam veniēs!"** (34:10–11)
> *"How gladly I will see him again! But of course I will see you much more gladly (more gladly by much) when you come to Rome!"*
> **Multīs post annīs . . . pervēnit.** (Exercise 37c, No. 3)
> *"He arrived . . . many years later (later by many years).*

4. With names of cities and the word **domus,** the idea of *place from which* is expressed by the ablative case without a preposition (see pages 80–81):

> **Brundisiō . . . proficīscētur. . . .** (34:8)
> *He will set out from Brundisium. . . .*
> **Domō profectus est.** (page 81)
> *He set out from home.*

E. Locative Case

The *locative case* is used to indicate *place where* with names of cities and the word **domus** (see pages 80–91):

> **Rōmae** at Rome, **Brundisiī** at Brundisium, **Carthāginī** at Carthage, **Bāiīs** at Baiae, and **domī** at home

II. ADJECTIVES

A. Adjectives occur in *positive*, *comparative*, and *superlative* degrees (see pages 45–47 and 51). For an example of a comparative adjective, see I.D.3 above, and for an example of a superlative adjective, see I.B.1 above.

Instead of following the rules given on pages 45–47, a few adjectives form their comparative and superlative degrees with the adverbs **magis** and **maximē**:

> **Paulātim igitur fiēbat magis ēbrius?**
> Exercise 32e, line 21)
> *Did he therefore gradually become more drunk?*
> **Statim factus est maximē ēbrius.** . . .
> (Exercise 32e, line 22)
> *Suddenly he became very drunk.*

Comparative adjectives may be used with **quam** or with the ablative case to express the comparison (see pages 47 and 51):

> **"Quis enim est prūdentior quam Gāius?"** (32:9–10)
> or **"Quis enim est prūdentior Gāiō?"**
> *"For who is wiser than Gaius?"*
> **Martiālis Eucleide est prūdentior.** (Exercise 33d, No. 4)
> or **Martiālis est prūdentior quam Eucleidēs.**
> *Martial is wiser than Eucleides.*

Superlative adjectives may be used with the *partitive genitive*, see I.B.1 above.

III. ADVERBS

A. Adverbs occur in *positive*, *comparative*, and *superlative* degrees (see pages 52–53). For an example of a comparative adverb, see I.D.3 above, and for an example of a superlative adverb, see I.B.1 above.

The comparative adverb may be used with **quam** or with the ablative case:

> **Nēmō celerius quam frāter meus currere potest.** (Exercise 33g, No. 3)
> *No one is able to run faster than my brother.*
> **Sextus celerius Marcō currere potest.** (Exercise 33g, No. 4)
> *Sextus is able to run faster than Marcus.*

Superlative adverbs may be used with the *partitive genitive* (see I.B.1 above).

V. VERBS

A. Verbs may be either *active* or *passive* in voice. In the active voice the subject is the *doer* of the action of the verb; in the passive voice the subject is the *receiver* of the action of the verb (see pages 15–16, 21–22, and 28–29):

> **Incolae omnia agunt.** (*active*, page 15)
> *The tenants are doing everything.*
> **Ab incolīs omnia aguntur.** (*passive*, page 15)
> *Everything is being done by the tenants.*

B. Some verbs, called *deponent*, are passive in form but active in meaning (see pages 64–65):

> **Subitō collāpsus est.** (32:27)
> *Suddenly he collapsed.*

C. Sometimes a writer will switch to the *present tense* while describing *past events*; this is called the *vivid* or *historic present* and helps make the reader feel personally involved in the narrative (see page 6).

D. The *imperfect tense* with **iam** and an expression of duration of time is often best translated in English with a pluperfect:

> **Iam multōs diēs in scaphā erāmus cum ā mercātōribus quibusdam inventī sumus.** (40:41–42)
> *We had already been in the boat for many days when we were found by certain merchants.*

E. The verb **placeō** is often used impersonally with the dative case:

> **Placuitne tibi cēna, Gāī?** (Exercise 32e, line 3)
> *Did the dinner please you, Gaius?* better English, *Did you like the dinner, Gaius?*

V. PARTICIPLES

A. Present Participles (see pages 88–90)
1. *Participles* are *verbal adjectives* and may modify nouns:

> **Nunc cōnspicit poētam versūs recitantem.** (27:18–19)
> *Now she catches sight of a poet reciting verses.*

Since the participle is a *verbal adjective*, it may take a *direct object* of its own; in the sentence above **versūs** is the object of the participle **recitantem**.

2. Present active participles are frequently used as *substantives* (nouns) (see page 89):

> **"Cavēte!" exclāmant adstantēs.** . . . (27:23–24)
> *"Watch out!" shout the bystanders.* . . .

B. Perfect Participles
1. *Perfect passive participles* often modify the subject of the verb of the clause or sentence (see pages 34–35):

> **Itaque coquus vocātus ab omnibus laudātus est.** (31:31)

Therefore the cook, <u>having been summoned</u>, was praised by everyone. (See page 34.)

2. The *perfect participle of a deponent verb* has an active meaning and is often best translated as a present participle (see page 65):

> . . . inde <u>regressus</u> . . . in hortō labōrābam. (38:6–7)
> *. . . <u>having returned</u> (returning) from there . . . I worked in the garden.*

VI. SENTENCES

A. Subordinate clauses are parts of sentences that cannot stand by themselves but are joined to the main clause by a variety of conjunctions, pronouns, and adverbs.

1. A new conjunction you have met in Book 3 that introduces subordinate clauses is **quoniam**:

> **Quoniam** neque cibum neque aquam habēbāmus, graviter aegrōtābāmus. (42:42–43)
> *<u>Since</u> we had neither food nor water, we became seriously ill.*

2. The relative pronoun (**quī, quae, quod**) introduces a relative clause and agrees with its antecedent in number and gender; its case depends on its use in its own clause (see page 7):

> Servī ā <u>quibus</u> lectīca ferēbātur ingentēs erant. (page 7)
> *The slaves by <u>whom</u> the litter was being carried were huge.*

The relative pronoun **quibus** is masculine and plural because of the gender and number of its antecedent, **servī**; it is ablative because of its use as the object of the preposition **ā** in its own clause.

> Omnia <u>quae</u> videt Cornēlia eam dēlectant. (27:18)
> *Everything <u>that</u> Cornelia sees pleases her.*

The relative pronoun **quae** is neuter and plural because of the gender and number of its antecedent, **omnia**; it is accusative because of its use as the direct object of **videt** in its own clause.

> ". . . īre ad mercātōrem quendam <u>cuius</u> taberna nōn procul abest. . ." (17:11–12)
> *". . . to go to a certain merchant <u>whose</u> shop is not far away. . . . "*

The relative pronoun **cuius** is masculine and singular because of the gender and number of its antecedent, **mercātōrem quendam**; it is genitive because of its use within its own clause.

3. Many subordinate clauses have their verbs in the *subjunctive* (see page 95), a form of the verb that will be presented fully in Book 4. In Book 3 you have met sentences such as the following:

> Grammaticus tamen, <u>cum</u> ego ignōrārem, īrā commōtus, ferulam rapuit et mē crūdēlissimē verberāvit. (38:22–23)
> *The teacher, however, <u>since</u> I <u>did not know</u> (the answer), moved with anger, seized his cane and beat me very cruelly.*

> . . . <u>cum</u> omnēs <u>dormīrent</u>, ego surrēxī. . . . 40:32)
> *. . . <u>when</u> all <u>were asleep</u>, I got up. . . .*

> Cornēlia, <u>cum</u> hoc <u>audīvisset</u>, maximē gaudēbat. . . . (39:18)
> *Cornelia, <u>when</u> she <u>had heard</u> this, was very glad. . . .*

> . . . etiam Aenēās ipse ignōrābat <u>ubi</u> <u>esset</u> Hesperia!" (38:21–22)
> *Even Aeneas himself did not know <u>where</u> Hesperia <u>was</u>!*

> . . . pīrātae . . . rogābant . . . <u>unde</u> <u>vēnissēmus</u>. . . . (40:21–22)
> *. . . the pirates asked <u>from where</u> we <u>had come</u>. . . .*

Cumulative Review of Books 1–2

PART 1: IN THE FORUM

Activity CR1a

Read aloud and translate:

Hodiē, quod occupātī sunt et Cornēlius et Titus, Eucleidēs ipse puerōs et Cornēliam in urbem dūcet. "Eugepae!" clāmat Sextus. "Ostendēsne nōbīs Forum atque aedificia?"

"Ita vērō," respondet Eucleidēs, "imprīmīs illa aedificia quae—" 5

Nōn licuit tamen Eucleidī rem explicāre, quod puerī iam tum ē domō exierant et per viās urbis praecurrēbant. Necesse erat Eucleidī et Cornēliae festīnāre. Mox ad Forum advēnērunt ubi Eucleidēs et Cornēlia puerōs prope arcum Tiberiī inveniunt. "Hic est arcus," inquit Eucleidēs, "ubi pater vester heri nōbīs occurrit. Imperātor Tiberius hunc arcum—" 10

"Ecce," interpellāvit Sextus, "quālis statua est illa?" 15

Marcus puerō magnō rīsū respondit, "Nōn est statua, stultissime! Ille est umbilīcus orbis terrārum."

"Ita vērō," inquit Cornēlia. "Est mīliārium aureum, quod Caesar Augustus aedificāvit." 20

Sextus tamen nōn audiēbat, sed subitō, "Age, Marce!" inquit et per Viam Sacram currēbat. Ubi Eucleidēs tandem puerōs cōnsecūtus est, Sextus eum rogāvit, "Quid est illud aedificium?" 25

"Illa est Basilica Iūlia," respondit Eucleidēs.

"Aedificāvitne basilicam Iūlius Caesar?" rogāvit Sextus. 30

"Ita vērō," respondit Eucleidēs, "Dīvus Iūlius hanc basilicam aedificāvit atque tōtum—" Sextus tamen iterum praecurrerat.

Multās hōrās puerī et puella Eucleidem per urbem dūcēbant. Multa dē aedificiīs rogābant. Decimā hōrā tandem domuī appropinquābant. Nōndum tamen erat tempus cēnāre; līberī igitur ad hortum cucurrērunt, Eucleidēs ad cubiculum. 35

      imprīmīs, especially
      umbilīcus orbis terrārum, the center of the
        universe

      orbis, orbis (*m*), circle, ring
      terra, -ae (*f*), earth, land
      mīliārium aureum, the golden milestone
      cōnsecūtus est, (he) overtook
      Basilica Iūlia, the Basilica Julia, one of
        Rome's law courts
      dīvus, -a, -um, divine
      multās hōrās, for many hours

Activity CR1b

Match each word at the left (taken from the designated line in the reading passage above) first with its case and then with its use within the phrase or sentence in which it occurs:

1.	puerōs (2)	A.	Vocative	a.	subject	
2.	aedificia (4)	B.	Nominative	b.	direct object	
3.	rem (7)	C.	Genitive			
4.	puerī (8)	D.	Dative	c.	indirect object	
5.	domō (8)	E.	Accusative			
6.	urbis (9)	F.	Ablative	d.	object of preposition	
7.	arcum (12)					
8.	hic (12)			e.	time	
9.	puerō (17)			f.	possession	
10.	rīsū (17)			g.	direct address	
11.	orbis (18–19)					
12.	terrārum (19)			h.	without preposition	
13.	Marce (23)					
14.	basilicam (29)					
15.	hōrās (34)					
16.	urbem (35)					
17.	aedificiīs (35)					
18.	hōrā (36)					

Activity CR1c

Change every noun in Exercise CR1b above that is not a proper noun to its plural form if it is singular and to its singular form if it is plural. Be sure to keep the same case.

Activity CR1d

*Modify the nouns listed in Exercise CR1b (excepting, again, the proper nouns) with the correct forms of the adjectives **parvulus, -a, -um** and **ingēns, ingentis**.*

Activity CR1e

Modify the nouns you used in Exercise CR1d above with the correct forms of the demonstrative adjectives **hic, haec, hoc** and **ille, illa, illud.**

Activity CR1f

Write out all forms of the following seven nouns from the story:

1. basilicam (32)
2. umbilīcus (18)
3. aedificium (26)
4. pater (13)
5. tempus (37)
6. arcus (12)
7. rem (7)

Activity CR1g

Translate the following phrases into English. Then rewrite the phrases by making all singular nouns plural and all plural nouns singular. Make sure you keep the nouns in the same case:

1. ē manibus
2. sub lapide
3. per viās
4. sine custōde
5. dē somniō mīlitis
6. prope mētam
7. intrā aedificia
8. cum mulieribus
9. ā portā
10. in lectīcās
11. ad amphitheātrum
12. post cēnam

Activity CR1h

Translate the following phrases into Latin without using prepositions:

1. at dawn
2. for us
3. at home
4. to the poets
5. with a great uproar
6. by a sign
7. for the soldier
8. to me
9. homeward
10. by the heat
11. for Cornelius
12. to Aurelia

PART 2: TO THE RACES AGAIN

Activity CR2a

Read aloud and translate:

Iam quīnta hōra erat. Hodiē, quod Cornēlius iterum ad Cūriam īverat et Eucleidēs aberat, licuit Titō Sextum et Marcum et Cornēliam ad Circum Maximum dūcere. Līberī cum patruō iam Montem Palātīnum circumierant et Circō appropinquābant. 5

"Eugepae," identidem clāmābat Sextus, quī aurīgās spectāre valdē volēbat, "hodiē nostrī russātī certē victōriam habēbunt."

"Ego," inquit Titus, "prasinīs semper faveō." 10

"Ego quoque prasinīs hodiē faveō," respondit Marcus, quod patruum valdē amābat.

Cornēlia tamen, "Ego adhūc venetīs faveō."

Ubi Circum intrāverant, Marcus Titum 15 rogāvit, "licetne nōbīs, patrue, prope arēnam sedēre?"

"Estō," inquit Titus, quī prope arēnam cum amīcīs suīs sedēre solēbat. "Nisi prope arēnam consēderimus, prīncipem numquam 20 cōnspiciēmus."

"Aut aurīgās," mussāvit Sextus, quī Titum bene nōvit.

"Aut bellās puellās," respondit Marcus, quī Titum melius nōvit. 25

Marcus et Sextus et Cornēlia multōs cursūs vidēre poterant. Aliās prasinī, aliās russātī victōriam habent. Saepissimē tamen victōriam habent venetī. Subitō homō quīdam Marcum ā tergō laesit. "Heus tū," exclāmat 30 Marcus, "Cavē! Nōlī mē laedere! Sī tū fīliō senātōris nocueris, pater meus tē certē—"

"Tacē, Marce," interpellāvit Titus. "Nōlī illum hominem vexāre! Praetereā, tempus est nōbīs domum īre. Pater vester nōs exspec- 35 tābit."

Titus igitur līberōs invītōs ē Circō domum per viās urbis dūxit.

nōvit, (he) knew
bene, well
bellus, -a, -um, beautiful
melius, better
cursus, -ūs (*m*), race
aliās, sometimes
saepissimē, most often
ā tergō, from behind
Heus! Hey!
   laedō, laedere (3), **laesī, laesum,** to knock, strike

Activity CR2b

Identify the tense, person, and number of the following verbs (taken from the designated line of the reading passage above). Then write the principal parts of each verb:

1. aberat (3)
2. circumierant (5–6)
3. volēbat (8)
4. habēbunt (9)
5. faveō (11)

6. intrāverant (15)
7. cōnspiciēmus (20–21)
8. mussāvit (22)
9. poterant (27)
10. laesit (30)
11. nocueris (32)

1. cōgitās
2. docēbimus
3. circumībāmus
4. puniētis
5. scīvistis
6. pervēneris
7. sūmpserō
8. nārrābam
9. vetō
10. nocuerātis
11. coniēcistī
12. iēcerāmus

Activity CR2c

Using the same verbs listed in Exercise CR2b above, write out the remaining five tenses of the verb, keeping the same person and number.

Activity CR2d

Complete the following sentences by filling in each blank with a present infinitive. Make sure your sentence makes sense. Then translate the sentences into English:

1. Sextus omnia aedificia in urbis _____ volēbat.
2. Cornēlia hodiē ad Circum Maximum _____ nōn vult.
3. Puerī ad mediam noctem _____ in animō habuērunt.
4. Nōs sine custōde in urbem _____ timēbāmus.
5. Ego vōs in cubiculīs _____ iussī.
6. Potesne fābulam mīlitis mihi _____?
7. Licet nōbīs hīc _____.

Activity CR2e

Give the imperatives of the following verbs, singular and plural:

1. cōgitāre
2. pūnīre
3. dūcere
4. ferre
5. dare
6. venīre
7. nōlle
8. pōnere

Activity CR2f

Give the other principal parts of the following verbs:

1. surgō
2. inventum
3. vidēre
4. trādidī
5. cadere
6. sūmō
7. ēgī
8. lātum
9. aedificāvī
10. fīnīre
11. occurrō
12. relictum
13. trāxī
14. apertum
15. vetuī
16. faveō

Activity CR2g

Give the proper personal pronoun to match the ending of each verb:

Activity CR2h

Match each verb form at the left with its proper translation:

1. vīdit
2. ferēbās
3. vīderat
4. pūnīvimus
5. tulistī
6. pūnīverāmus
7. vidēbat
8. fers
9. vīderit
10. pūniverimus
11. ferēs
12. tulerās
13. pūniēmus
14. tuleris
15. pūnīmus
16. videt
17. vidēbit
18. pūniēbāmus

a. we have punished
b. he had seen
c. we are punishing
d. you will bring
e. you carry
f. we had punished
g. he sees
h. you brought
i. she will see
j. we will punish
k. we began to punish
l. she will have seen
m. you had brought
n. we will have punished
o. he saw
p. she used to see
q. you will have brought
r. you were carrying

Activity CR2i

List three compound verbs formed from the following verbs. Give all principal parts for each compound:

1. dūcō
2. faciō
3. eō
4. sum
5. ferō
6. cēdō
7. iaciō
8. veniō

Activity CR2j

Make up six Latin sentences, using the six irregular verbs listed below. Each sentence should use a different tense of the six you have learned, as well as a different person or number:

1. sum
2. possum
3. volō
4. nōlō
5. ferō
6. eō